MW00379444

SHOUTS FROM THE WALL:

Posters and Photographs
Brought Home From
the Spanish Civil War
by American Volunteers

BY CARY NELSON

A Catalogue to Accompany the Exhibit
Curated by Peter Carroll and Cary Nelson for the Abraham
Lincoln Brigade Archives

DISTRIBUTED BY THE UNIVERSITY OF ILLINOIS PRESS

Cary Nelson is Jubilee Professor of Liberal Arts and Sciences
at the University of Illinois at Urbana–Champaign.

The Abraham Lincoln Brigade Archives welcomes inquires
(at its Brandeis University address) about all its activities.

FRONT COVER: Renau; *VICTORY—TODAY MORE THAN EVER*
BACK COVER [ABOVE]: Sim; *SHE SAW HIM FALL*
BACK COVER [BELOW]: Sim; *AFTER THE STRUGGLE*

Published by the Abraham Lincoln Brigade Archives
Box LII–Brandeis University–Waltham, Massachusetts 02254

designed by Michael Herbert and Dawn Hachenski

Contents

AIXAFEM FEIXISME *SMASH FASCISM*
Pere Català Roca [1936]

INTRODUCTION

*Spain tore the earth with her nails
When Paris was most beautiful.
Spain poured out her enormous tree of blood
When London tended its gardens and its lake of swans.
—Pablo Neruda*

Shouts from the Wall: Posters and Photographs Brought Back from the Spanish Civil War by American Volunteers opens a three-year tour at the Puffin Room in Manhattan in April 1996. The exhibition and tour are made possible by grants to the Abraham Lincoln Brigade Archives from the Puffin Foundation, the Charles Lawrence Keith and Clara Miller Foundation, the Program for Cultural Cooperation Between Spain's Ministry of Culture and United States Universities, the Blue Mountain Center, and the Needmor Fund. We thank all these donors for their vision and support. In the case of Perry Rosenstein and Gladys Miller-Rosenstein of the Puffin Foundation, thanks is not enough. We must also honor their friendship and their ongoing support throughout this project. Professional services have been provided by the Technical Assistance Program, a division of the American Federation of Arts.

*Sometimes I wake at night
out of completest sleep
and see their remembered faces
luminous in the dark.
Ghostly as tracer-bullets
their smiles, their hesitant speech,
their eloquent hands in gesture
and their smiles belying fear:
Antonio, Catalan,
eighteen years old ... Hilario ...
—Edwin Rolfe*

Founded in 1975, The Abraham Lincoln Brigade Archives (ALBA) is a nonprofit national organization devoted to the preservation and dissemination of the record of the American role in the 1936–39 Spanish Civil War and its aftermath. ALBA supervises a major archive at Brandeis University—the most comprehensive historical archive documenting the American involvement in the Spanish Civil War—and supports cultural and educational activities related to the war and its historical, political, artistic, and biographical heritage. In addition to this catalogue and exhibit, ALBA's major recent activities include: the acquisition of microfilm copies of the massive International Brigades Archives from the Russian Center for the Preservation and Study of Documents of Recent History in Moscow; sponsorship of the George Watt Fund, an annual contest for the best student essays written about the Spanish Civil War; sponsorship of conferences and production of books about the Spanish Civil War. Following standard usage since 1937, we use the term "Lincoln Brigade" in our organization's title to honor all the Americans who came to the aid of the Spanish Republic from 1936–1939. In actuality there was an Abraham Lincoln Battalion, not brigade, but Americans served in other battalions and in the medical corps and transport regiment as well.

This exhibit was assembled by Cary Nelson and Peter Carroll, both members of the Abraham Lincoln Brigade Archives Executive Committee. We have had continual consultation from our fellow Executive Committee member William Susman, a veteran of the Spanish Civil War. The exhibit could not have been mounted without the long-term help of our Brandeis University archivist Victor Berch and without regular advice from our fellow ALBA Board member Andrew Lee of New York University's Tamiment library. Special thanks goes to Nick Chapman for sending me a copy of his undergraduate thesis on Spanish Civil War posters; it is one of the best essays written on the subject. Other assistance came from the Director of Special Collections at Brandeis University, Charles Cutter, and from Leon Chai, Juan Sola-Montserrat, and Robin Ragan at the University of Illinois and Patty Roberts at Centenary College. Except for four posters from the Rare Books and Special Collections Division at the University of Illinois at Urbana-Champaign (nos. 21 and 23– 25), all the posters come from the Abraham Lincoln Brigades Archive at Brandeis University. We thank ALBA Board member Bessie Hahn of Brandeis and Robert Wedgeworth of the University of Illinois for their assistance. We cannot be certain how the University of Illinois posters were first acquired, but we know how ALBA's posters came to the United States: they were mailed or carried home by Americans who risked their lives helping to defend the Spanish Republic from 1936 to 1939. Those 2,800 Americans came from all over the country and from almost every imaginable occupation. Most were communists; some were liberal democrats or socialists. All were anti– fascists; that conviction and sense of historical necessity unified them and kept them dedicated despite facing overwhelmingly superior military equipment on the other side. These Americans had read the future accurately; they knew that the world was in peril from fascism.

Only a few months before Americans began arriving in Spain, the country had held democratic elections that installed a new progressive coalition government. The losing conservative parties decided they would not accept the people's vote. They began to plot a coup, and in July 1936 their allies among the most reactionary military leaders attempted to take control of the country. In the major cities of Spain the people rose up to crush the revolt. But Europe's fascist dictators—Germany's Hitler, Italy's Mussolini, and Portugal's Salazar—offered the rebel generals military assistance at the moment their cause seemed lost. Then, in an alternative victory strategy, Franco sent four columns of troops toward the capital city, hoping to overwhelm Madrid and win the war in one decisive maneuver. He did not succeed. Instead, both Spaniards and the international volunteers who came to their aid would face repeated battles around the capital in the fall and winter of 1936–37, followed, among other campaigns, by the furnace of Brunete in the summer heat of 1937, by the frozen battle of Teruel in the winter of 1937–38, and by the massive Ebro campaign in the summer of 1938.

Had Hitler and Mussolini not rapidly offered Spain's rebel generals men and arms, the Spanish Civil War would have remained a short-lived internal conflict, instead of a war lasting over two and a half years with broad international implications. The people of Spain would have crushed the military rebellion against their democratically elected government, and the fascist powers would not have had so decisive an opportunity to test the resolve of the Western democracies. Unfortunately, the test did take place, and the West failed it when it adopted a policy of appeasement, refusing to sell arms to the Republic while Germany and Italy generously armed the rebel leader Francisco Franco. Only Mexico and the Soviet Union sold arms to the Republic, but those arms, which had to travel great distances at considerable peril, were finally no match for the fascists' supplies. Had the West stood firm against fascism in Spain, the history of our century might read somewhat differently.

Because the Spanish Civil War was, in effect, the opening battle of the Second World War, because it was the first time the world experienced saturation bombing of civilian targets, because the 40,000 volunteers from fifty–two countries who joined the International Brigades did so in selfless dedication to the common good: for all these and other reasons it holds a special place in modern history. No other conflict in this century has combined the drama, the historical importance, and the ethical clarity of the struggle between democracy and fascism. Spain was its first major phase. But it was also unique, in that almost all the volunteer soldiers had a deep understanding of why they were there. These posters thus form a major part of the visual record of one of the major cultural, philosophical, moral, political, and military conflicts of modern history. They deserve to be understood and valued in that context.

The Americans who brought these posters home have had a special status in the culture of the Left for sixty years. They remain living emblems of what it means to place the public good above your own welfare, to risk everything in pursuit of a better world. As the International Brigades were preparing to leave Spain in October of 1938, the Republic's most admired orator, La Pasionaria, sought to state for the record what the gift of their lives had meant:

You came to us from all peoples, from all races. You came like brothers of ours, like sons of undying Spain; and in the hardest days of the war, when the capital of the Spanish Republic was threatened, it was you, gallant comrades of the International Brigades, who helped to save the city with your fighting enthusiasm, your heroism and your spirit of sacrifice . . . . In deathless verses Jarama and Guadalajara, Brunete and Belchite, Levante and the Ebro sing the courage, the self–sacrifice, the daring, the discipline of the men of the International Brigades . . . . And they asked us for nothing at all . . . they did aspire to the honor of dying for us . . . . You can go proudly. You are history. You are legend. You are the heroic example of democracy's solidarity and universality . . . .

Almost fifty years later the novelist and film maker John Sayles also sought to pay tribute to the uncannily haunting inspiration the men and women of the International Brigades, among them the Lincolns, continue to provide: "They fought," he wrote in 1986," when they didn't have to fight, fought when it brought no public glory in their home towns, fought to put a lie to the cynicism that keeps people in darkness. They won't go away. The example of their sacrifice stands up in history for those of us not yet born when they shipped out for a Republic that was mostly a belief in what people could be, in how they could live together. And in a world run by cynics, in a time when caring about someone you've never met is seen as weakness or treachery, how much strength have we taken from the thought of them, how much pride and comfort to be able to say, `But what about the guys in the Lincoln Brigade?'" We mean this exhibit and its accompanying catalogue to pay tribute to them and to the history they witnessed and helped to make.

THE HERMAPHRODITIC LITHOGRAPHIC VERSION OF RAMÓN PUYOL'S **EL RUMOR**
[AUTHORS COLLECTION]

Ramón Puyol

A SPANISH CIVIL WAR CHRONOLOGY

EMPHASIZING AMERICAN VOLUNTEERS

1936

February 16	Popular Front coalition of left—wing parties wins Spanish national elections and forms new Republican government
July 18	Right—wing military uprising against the Spanish government
July 19	Insurgents are defeated as they attempt to take Barcelona
July 20	Insurgents defeated in Madrid; Franco takes control of Insurgent armies
July 25	Hitler agrees to support Franco
July 27	Insurgents control Seville with reinforcements flown in from Morocco on German airplanes
September 9	The Non—Intervention Committee first meets in London
November 6	Republican government leaves Madrid and moves to Valencia; General Miaja named head of Madrid Defense Junta
November 7–23	Insurgents attack Madrid from the north and southwest
November 8	International Brigades arrive in Madrid
November 18	Germany and Italy recognize Nationalist government
December 22	Italian forces arrive in Spain to support Insurgents
December 25	The first Americans leave New York harbor on the S. S. Normandie to fight for the Republic

1937

February 5–27	Battle of Jarama
February 27	Lincolns attack Pingarrón Hill ("Suicide Hill") in Jarama Valley; of the 500 who went over the top, more than 300 were killed or wounded
February 8	Nationalists capture Malaga

March 8–18	Battle of Guadalajara; Italian troops defeated by Republican army with substantial International Brigade support	
March–May	Americans form two new battalions—the George Washington Battalion and the MacKenzie-Papineau Battalion (consisting mostly of Canadians)	
May 3–8	Fighting in Barcelona between CNT, FAI, POUM, and the PSUC and police	
April 26	Guernica bombed by German planes; over 2,500 civilian casualties	
July 6–26	Republican offensive at Battle of Brunete, just west of Madrid	
July 6	Lincolns attack and take Villanueva de la Cañada near Brunete; 30 Lincolns killed	
July 9	Lincolns charge the Romanillos Heights and Mosquito Crest ("Mosquito Hill"); over 135 casualties; they dig in and are bombarded by the German Condor Legion	
July 14	Because of high casualties the Lincoln and Washington Battalions merge into one battalion	
August 24	Republican offensive in Aragón; the Lincolns attack Quinto	
September 6	Belchite, falls to the Lincolns after 4 days of house–to–house fighting. The Lincolns suffer over 250 casualties in the battles of Quinto and Belchite	
October 13	Lincolns and the MacPaps unsuccessfully attack Fuentes de Ebro	
October 19	All of Northern Spain in Nationalist control	
November 30	Republican government moves to Barcelona	
December 14	Republican offensive begins at Teruel	

1938 **February 15** Lincolns and MacPaps sent to Segura de los Baños, about 70 kilometers north of Teruel; they take Monte Pedigrossa; Americans also in action elsewhere in the area

February 22	Nationalists recapture Teruel
March 10	Nationalists begin major offensive in Aragón; the Lincolns retreat south out of Belchite and are overrun by rebel offensive, with many taken prisoner; the beginning of the Great Retreats
March 16–18	Continuous bombing of Barcelona
April 15	Nationalists break through Republican forces and reach Mediterranean at Vinaroz; Republican Spain split in two
July 24	Republican army begins Ebro offensive; the Lincolns cross the river near Asco and quickly take Fatarella
August 2	Lincolns just east of Gandesa; pounded by artillery in the "Valley of Death"
September 21	Juan Negrín, Prime Minister of the Republic, announces to the League of Nations at Geneva a unilateral withdrawal of all international troops from the Republican army; the Lincolns are near the front lines just east of Corbera
September 24	The Lincolns are withdrawn from the Ebro region
September 30	Munich Pact seals fate of Czechoslovakia, and of Spain's last chance for intervention; Neville Chamberlain declares "Peace in our time"
October 29	Farewell parade in Barcelona for the International Brigades
December 2	Over 300 Americans cross over into France
1939 **January 26**	Nationalists capture Barcelona
March 27	Nationalists take over Madrid
April 1	Franco declares war ended
September 1	Hitler invades Poland; World War II begins

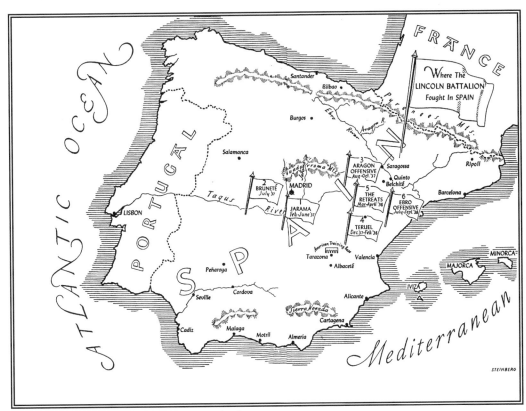

REPRINTED FROM EDWIN ROLFE, **THE LINCOLN BATTALION** [1939]

FROM THE PORTFOLIO **MI PATRIA SANGRA... ESTAMPAS DE LA INDEPENDENCIA DE ESPAÑA**
TO DEFEND THEIR LIBERTY

José Bardasano

FROM THE PORTFOLIO **MI PATRIA SANGRA... ESTAMPAS DE LA INDEPENDENCIA DE ESPAÑA**
EXODUS

José Bardasano

ART IN FLAMES: THE SPANISH CIVIL WAR POSTER

CARY NELSON

> *Jan. 7.*
> *Barcelona beautiful.*
> *Streets aflame with posters*
> *of all parties for all causes,*
> *some of them put out*
> *by combinations*
> *of parties.[1]*

So wrote American volunteer Robert Merriman in his diary when he arrived in Spain at the beginning of 1937. Full-color posters, banners, and fliers, brandishing dramatic swaths of red and black or blue or yellow were all over the city: along the streets, taped to windows, tacked up on kiosks in every public square, on the interior walls of office buildings and private homes, in all the subway stations, on the sides of buses, trucks, and even trains. By the second week of the war, early in July 1936, they were already defining the public space of major cities. *Daily Worker* correspondent George Marion, writing to *Time* magazine on his return home—his March 1st, 1938, letter is unpublished but a copy is in his file at the Abraham Lincoln Brigade Archives—reported that "the posters flow from a hundred sources. During the many months I was in Spain I found the collection of posters just about a full-time job because there was no central source."[2] Many, he continued, were "put out by non-governmental bodies: trade unions, youth organizations, women's committee, Fifth Regiment, and others." On the Puerto del Sol, central square of Madrid, one huge poster on the side of a building occupied a whole floor. Soon they appeared on bulletin boards and at headquarters at the fronts where men were fighting. They gave people information they needed, built morale, and focused debate and action on the key issues and campaigns of a given week. Communication, exhortation, persuasion, instruction, celebration, warning: all these aims and more were served by the 1,500 to 2,000 different posters appearing in the Spanish Republic from 1936–38. Of this number, perhaps 20 percent were exclusively textual; the rest of the posters were preeminently pictorial.

They were first of all an excellent mode of communication for a population with a high rate of illiteracy. For many years, Spain's Catholic church, in control of public education, believed there was no need for either peasants or women to read. The Republic would begin rapidly to reverse that pattern, but in the meantime posters in public places combining striking iconography with brief slogans made it possible to get basic messages out to people quickly. The combination of strong graphics with concise captions also made the posters memorable and convincing.

---

[1] The passages taken from Robert Merriman's diary and from letters by Dave Gordon and Leon Rosenthal are quoted from Cary Nelson and Jefferson Hendricks, eds. *Madrid 1937: Letters of the Abraham Lincoln Brigade from the Spanish Civil War*. The originals of these documents remain in the possession of family members, but we were permitted to photocopy them.

[2] Marion signed the letter with his pseudonym "James Hawthorne."

Early on large numbers of them were essentially recruitment posters. Carles Fontseré's *Al Front* urged everyone to turn their eyes and their full attention to the rapidly expanding war; its helmeted soldier negotiated all the extremes of light and dark in such a way as to suggest there was no world outside the imperiled horizon of battle. In the presence of this icon there might seem no alternative but to volunteer. So too with José Bardasano's *España*. All available and politically relevant nobility is combined in its lion's confident stance and gaze of warm concern; stand with honor, the poster urges us, and give yourself over to be gathered into the country's protective vigilance. These highly general inducements to solidarity and commitment were balanced with special pleas for particular militias. "Workers!" declared one of J. Bauset's posters, "joining the Iron Column fortifies the revolution." The iron column was an anarchist battalion, but other militias had their recruitment posters as well. In such cases, moreover, the posters went beyond literal recruitment. They amounted to ideological recruitment, urging people to place their faith and their loyalty with a particular political point of view.

In these first months of the war there were also a series of gendered posters. Spanish women were urged to join the militias, to take up arms with men and boys. Even now, these images, including Sim's remarkable portraits of armed women in battle, have the power to surprise us. By spring 1937, however, it became clear to many that the militias would not suffice to fight large-scale battles in a prolonged war; a centrally organized army was required to meet coordinated attacks by columns of infantry, tanks, and planes. Meanwhile, the army needed to increase its size as well, thereby leaving behind fewer men to keep Spain's industries running. Women were not sent back to the home, their traditional site in Spain, but they disappeared from combat as the militias were dissolved; instead, posters appearing from mid–1937 on urged them to take up the slack in industry and agriculture. Juan Antonio's *Women, Work for the Comrades Who Fight* is a good example of that sort of poster, as is a poster jointly designed by Juana Francisco and José Bardasano, *Our Arms Will Be Yours*. One of the most telling pieces of visual evidence of the disappearance of women from combat is Sim's second portfolio of drawings, *12 Escenas de Guerra*. In his first collection of battle illustrations, *Estampas de la Revolucion Española 19 Julio de 1936*, women are portrayed in about half of the illustrations; *12 Escenas de Guerra* is devoted entirely to men. His first portfolio, notably, was published by the anarchists. The second collection was issued by the central government, the Generalitat, of Catalonia. The second collection also uses less vibrant color, emphasizing the brown uniforms of the regular army rather than the red and black colors of anarchism.

LES MILICIES, US NECESSITEN!
THE MILITIAS NEED YOU!
Arteche

Throughout the war there were poster campaigns focused on particular needs and events. Thus when the Asturias were overrun by Franco's troops posters like Cheché's *Aid The Families of the Fighters of the North* helped focus public attention on the plight of the refugees. Continuing problems, like the perennial one of soldiers getting drunk on leave, would also be the focus of special publicity campaigns; hence Artel's *A Drunk! He is aParasite! Eliminate Him!* Some issues and campaigns were the subject of posters throughout the war; the effort to promote literacy, one of the Republic's key social agendas, was one of these. Other topics received more intermittent treatment; these include ecological posters warning people cutting wood for heat about the dangers of deforestation. The last year of the war, when the Republic was losing territory to the fascists, saw a number of posters aiming to help build morale, stiffen resistance, and reinforce solidarity. Slogans like "Resist," "Counterattack," or "Fortify" identify a poster as produced in 1938 rather than 1937.

Our information about production methods for Spanish Civil War posters comes mainly from Carles Fontseré, the Catalan artist who was active in the Union of Professional Artists (*Sindicato de Dibujantes Profesionales*) in Barcelona. As he describes the process, a poster artist typically painted in water colors on moistened paper stretched across a frame. The verbal text was also painted by hand. In most cases, after the original poster was painted, a lithographer copied each color onto a separate zinc plate for printing. Some of the artists, however, including Fontseré, worked directly on the zinc plates themselves. The requirement for multiple plates worked against the use of too many colors; three or four was typical, five or six unusual.

A number of other material constraints also affected the posters. First, they had to be clearly visible from a distance in order to be effective in public sites, including outdoor locations. Second, the use of watercolors made it impractical to overpaint with light colors over dark ones. Instead, poster artists often used the white of the paper itself as a major design element. Finally, the paper used was generally the least expensive, often a form of newsprint. The largest number of posters were about 30 inches wide and forty inches high, though double-sized posters, printed on two sheets of this size and glued together were not uncommon, and some substantially larger posters were produced. Many posters were printed in runs of 5,000 or 10,000 copies, enough to guarantee wide distribution and visibility. The cities of Barcelona, Madrid, and Valencia each had two or more large poster workshops working continually. Usually a given workshop specialized in posters for a particular political group or coalition of groups.

Variations on the primary pattern included a number of small posters printed by photo–chromolithography on high quality paper and sold in streetside stalls, offices, and bookstores. Drawings and lithographs were also issued in more limited editions on heavy stock for sale to individual buyers. And some posters needed for immediate use in a particular place were done as unique paintings, sometimes in oil. Like similar workshops in Madrid and Valencia, the *Sindicato* also produced banners and placards. The banners were painted directly on primed cotton whenever it could be obtained.

A great many posters were also reprinted as postcards, sometimes many months later, so that a given image often received a second life and a second means of distribution. A considerable number of postcards were also independently designed and never appeared as posters. From time to time sets of ten postcards were sold in illustrated packets. Many thousands of such cards were sent home by international soldiers, journalists, and other visitors to Spain. Finally, small decorative stamps in substantial numbers—over a thousand different ones during the course of the war—were issued as miniature posters. Some reproduced large poster designs, but many represent independent works of art.

Fontseré has called the posters the "certificate" of the social revolution that formed in response to the generals' attempted coup: "each union, each small committee, came out with its poster; each profession, each trade–barbers, taxi drivers, tram conductors–could be seen in a poster breaking the bonds that oppressed them."

Inevitably, visitors and volunteers began sending the posters home; there was no more economical way to communicate the passion of the war. Here, on a single sheet typically thirty inches wide and forty high, was a powerful synecdoche for the war's anguish and its idealism—a woman holding a murdered child, the working classes looking up as they yearned for liberation, the archetypal soldier now taking a stand against the evil of fascism. Inevitably too, not only in Spain but across Europe and in America as well, exhibitions were mounted to give people a chance to see numbers of posters at once. Few at the time doubted that art and politics were here decisively fused, for the posters were both aesthetically beautiful or terrifying and politically compelling. They cried out to be seen and acted upon; between the two impulses no space of doubt need fall. If we have unlearned this lesson in the intervening years, the 60th anniversary of the start of the Spanish Civil War seems an appropriate occasion to have it displayed for a different generation.

When American volunteers wrote home about the posters they saw and sometimes sent back to friends and family, it was, often as not, an individual poster that would engage their attention. Leon Rosenthal, writing home in August, 1937, took some relish in comparing a friend back home to one of Ramón Puyol's satiric portraits: "As for Gershon—I wish I had the poster I would like to send him—it shows the super-leftist—with two arms on the right shoulder raised in 2 fists and one left one—and a fist for a nose, etc.,etc., and inside his belly is a fat bourgeois sitting on a soft chair & smoking a cigar." Dave Gordon, writing in July 1938, concentrated on a poster with little dramatic color but with a decisive cultural message:

> Who hasn't seen thousands of posters, whether for advertising or for propaganda? (Of course the advertising is only another type of propaganda itself.) Has there ever been a poster which did not contain a rather more than less obvious moral tailing along, either in the watchwords or catchwords or in the photograph, or drawing? It would be hard to find one which spoke for itself. It is extremely difficult to present the lesson desired without some concise wording or without plainly indicating the idea graphically. Yet this is exactly what was done in a poster issued by the Generalitat of Catalonia. What is more, this particular poster deals with the principal pride of Catalonia, with what so strongly characterizes its special individuality and comprehends all of its cultural traits—the Catalan language. Picture to yourself a photo-montage of two pages of a newspaper, one more and the other less obliquely reproduced on a huge poster sheet. Remember, too, that these newspaper pages are taken from a rebel fascist newspaper, impertinently bearing the name *Unidad*. The name "Catalonia" is printed in large letters, once at the head and once at the foot of the poster. Part of one of the

EL IZQUIERDISTA – EL EMBOSCADO SE CUBRE DE TODOS LOS ROPAJES PARA MEJOR ASESINAR EN LA SOMBRA! ANIQUILÉMOSLE SE ENCUENTRE DONDE SE ENCUENTRE!
THE ULTRALEFTIST—THE AMBUSHER WEARS MANY DISGUISES TO ASSASSINATE FROM UNDER COVER! WE ANNIHILATE HIM WHEREVER WE FIND HIM!
Ramón Puyol [1936–37]

newspapers is underscored in black. The underscored lines are only one sentence in a longer article. The paper is written in the Castilian tongue. The specially marked portion, translated, reads: "José Juan Jubert (fined) 100 pesetas and Javier Gibert Porrero, 100 pesetas, for speaking in Catalan at the table in the dining room of a hotel." The newspaper, published in San Sebastian, bears the date January 6th, 1938. The news item is a report of the court procedure of a day at the fascist tribunals. The poster carries no more than what I have explained above. Yet it speaks worlds. It reflects a profound confidence in the understanding and pride of the Catalan. At the same time it reveals a grand contempt for the dogs of fascism who aim to crush the culture of the regions of Spain. It is a convincing call to all Catalonia to fight with Spain to defeat fascism if it wishes to retain its freedoms. It is a simple poster, colored simply. I wish I had a copy to send you so that I need not have been compelled to describe it in words. It speaks most eloquently for itself. Yet I can't help writing about it for two reasons—it impressed me considerably and I could not get a copy of it.

There were new posters continually throughout the war and in time old ones would disappear from stores and be covered over on the streets with new issues. One of the most useful things to know would be the exact week that each poster was published. Definite proof would not always be available, but a search through daily newspapers and weekly magazines from 1936–39 could produce a list of poster reproductions; that would set latest dates of appearance for a number of posters. Also helpful would be a detailed chronology of wartime slogans and cultural campaigns; that would give likely dates for many of the posters bearing such slogans. Though there are many detailed military and political chronologies of the war, we lack a comparably detailed cultural chronology. Again, no one has yet done this research in Spanish publications, but it could be done. All this would enable far more precise readings of the posters than scholars have produced to date.

Even without being able to date and contextualize each poster, we can, however, give some overall feeling for the rich, mutually reinforcing semiotic environment in which many of the posters were displayed. Those that were published and displayed for particular week-long campaigns, for example, would have seemed not isolated objects to be noticed or ignored but rather part of city-wide activities and celebrations concentrated on a single topic. Thus a week-long campaign to build support for the Republic's new regular army was held throughout loyalist Spain in February 1937. Numerous posters were created for the occasion and displayed all along the streets. In Barcelona's *Plaza de Catalunya* a huge soldier designed by sculptor Miguel Paredes was constructed of wood, wire, and plaster of Paris. At the week's end a parade was held; as the army marched through Barcelona's *Paseo de Gracia* and *Plaza de Catalunya*, literally tens of thousands of volunteers held posters and placards aloft. Meanwhile numerous pamphlets and postcards were printed to supplement the posters, along with smaller decorations that people could attach to their clothing.

Large multifaceted cultural events focused on other week-long campaigns as well. A week of support for the Basque region, held from May 29 to June 6, 1937, brought out posters, banners, and placards with Basque motifs. A monument symbolizing the sacred tree of Guernica was erected in the *Plaza de Catalunya*, and the Basque play *Pedro Mari* was performed in the Liceo theater on Barcelona's Ramblas; poster artists designed the sets. The opening performance was interrupted by a bombing raid, but the cast and audience spurned the air raid shelters and stayed on singing the "Internationale." Later that summer a week advocating "Aid to Madrid" followed. That fall special celebrations to honor the International Brigades were held in Madrid. On September 5 a mass meeting adorned with posters and banners produced for the occasion was held in the Monumental Cinema. Posters advertising the meeting and other posters honoring the I.B. went up across the city. Pamphlets were issued about the event, as was a book of poems about the volunteer soldiers.

By no means all of the civil war posters were issued during these special campaigns; indeed, it would be purely speculative to estimate what percentage were. But one thing is true of almost all the posters: they require special annotation now if people are to decipher their special symbols and messages. In all of this Spanish Civil War poster scholarship is in its infancy. Indeed, in most cases the annotations provided here are the most detailed to be found anywhere. An emotional or aesthetic response to the image alone is an important part of any response we can have, but it does not suffice. Our understanding needs to be contextualized; we need to have some grasp of how the posters might have been read in their own political and historical moment. In some cases the iconography makes specific references that would have been obvious to contemporary Spaniards and would be utterly opaque to most of us now. This catalogue starts that process for the posters in this show. Writing comparable annotations for 1,500 posters would be a more daunting task, but at least the annotations here can be used as a guide for asking comparable questions of posters in other books or archives.

Equally problematic is the lack of biographical detail about the artists themselves. The research that should have taken place in Spain to establish at least the basic biographical facts about the Republican artists of the Spanish Civil War unfortunately could not begin until after Franco's death in 1975. By that time a number of the artists had no doubt died as well; many opportunities to interview artists or their friends or family have thus been lost. In any case, nothing was published in Spain about Republican posters until after 1975, and the books published about Civil War posters to date offer excellent general essays on the posters but include virtually no biographical information about the artists. In a number of cases no one has even established the artist's full name. Nonetheless, scattered information about several artists' lives does exist, and it is collated and published here for the first time in English. I concentrate on six figures—Bardasano, Fontseré, Francisca, Puyol, Renau, Sim—who are unquestionably among the most important poster artists of the war and four of whom are featured in the second section of the exhibit.

As scholars gather solid evidence about the specific dating of the posters and the careers of the artists it will be possible to take up a series of important issues that remain unresolved. Central among these is the question of stylistic development and changes in poster art over the course of the war. Clearly subject matter changes significantly from mid–1936 to the end of 1938, but does the style of the posters change as well? Some, including Carles Fontseré, have claimed that the most artistically inventive posters were done in 1936 and 1937, that by 1938 Spanish Civil War poster art had succumbed to dull uniformity and realism. Fontseré tends to blame this on the central government's increasing influence, but his is a highly interested political account. For those who romanticize the anarchist and POUMist militias, the increasing power of the central government in Catalonia, the move to a conventional army, and finally the growing influence of the Communist Party (a rather small group at the war's start) all combine to stifle spontaneity and promote conformity after the summer of 1937.

Yet Renau's "Victory" poster, a 1938 issue, seems a good counter example of fairly startling creativity. So too, in my opinion, do Giandante's 1938 poster sketches, many of them simultaneously issued as postcards. They are almost the 1938 equivalents of Sim's 1936 sketches of the people's resistance. Giandante did rapid ink sketches seeking a symbolic iconography of last resistance and solidarity. Hardly straightforwardly realistic or representational, his posters aim to capture the emotional core of a people under assault but united in purpose.

A number of artists remain steadfast in style and productivity throughout the war. Bardasano is a good example, producing posters in expressionist realism from 1936 to the end of 1938. On the other hand, there are artists whose style changes. Puyol stopped doing his surrealist portraits after 1937, and there is one Puyol poster in a flatly realist style dating from mid–1937, but Puyol had always worked in a variety of styles. So the issue is partly one of taste. If you do not admire Bardasano or Renau, if you find Giandante's poster sketches uninteresting, then you can easily say that no good work took place in the last year of the war. The issue then is partly what *count* as the most exciting posters. On the other hand, given the remarkable diversity of posters at all points in the war, it seems at best risky and anachronistic to impose our own aesthetic on such rich and complexly relational artistic products. The more abstract and symbolic posters were part of a relational field that included photographic posters, poster-sized cartoons, and posters from numerous modern traditions. Decorative, serialized art deco images coexisted in the public sphere with naive realism. All these styles to some degree spoke to one another and to an audience that processed and understood the war by way of these images.

Consider, for example, the range of posters focused on civilian anguish in the first year of the war. There are photographs of frightened women and children and of young bombing victims, and there are more symbolic, emotionally mediated painted icons of fear and anguish. Some photographic posters are almost flatly reportorial in their design, whereas others make use of collage or modernist dislocation. In Madrid and Barcelona, Valencia and Albacete, and in other towns and cities throughout the Republic one would have seen all these posters. One can imagine these different styles producing somewhat different responses and doing somewhat different sorts of cultural work. But nothing less than a representative selection of the total field of images can give us anything approximating the historical meaning of the posters. A certain catholicity of taste seems necessary, along with a willingness to seek contextualized knowledge. That is the way these images can speak to us most fully and powerfully.

FORTIFICAR
FORTIFY FOR VICTORY AND LIBERTY
Giandante [1938]

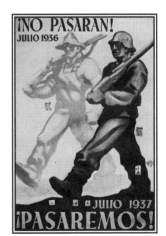

NO PASARÁN! JULIO
THEY SHALL NOT PASS! JULY 1936 WE SHALL NOT PASS! JULY 1937
Puyol [1937]

Before judging which poster of a dead child is most aesthetically successful, for example, we need to remember that virtually any Spanish resident of Madrid or Barcelona would have seen actual dead children on the street after air or artillery bombardments. They would then have seen comparable news photographs in newspapers and on pamphlets. The emotions they felt in the presence of real bodies and documentary photographs of real bodies would be carried into their response to the more mediated and stylized poster representations. The posters would concentrate and generalize those emotions, connecting them with abstract notions of injustice, violence, and beauty and with binary images of good and evil. The posters would give to anger and outrage and visceral shock or horror a certain aesthetic cast and make those emotions more available to political conviction and action. The posters, then, helped give direct experience broader cultural and historical meaning; moreover, they provided people with visual, emotional, and cultural icons that would serve as reference points in future bombing raids. Comparable wartime subject matter, in effect, recirculates through varying forms and contexts of representation. Even at a distance from Spain, there would be a difference between, say, a news photograph of bombing victims and Ras's bold, stylized poster of a mother holding her dead child. These complex negotiations between experience and multiple forms of representation are an inescapable part of the wartime meaning of these posters, and we cannot understand their historical meaning without reflecting on them.

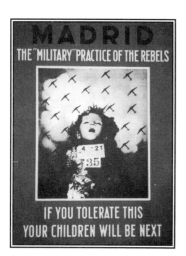

Anonymous

Writing shortly after the war was over, in his 1940 memoir *Freedom's Battle*, the Republic's foreign minister Julio Alvarez del Vayo recalls something of what these posters meant to their first audience:

> For some time the poster was one of the most effective mediums of propaganda. Its lesson was a visual one. In a country where—until such time as the Republican work of education began to bear fruit—a large part of the rural population was unable to read, the posters took the place of the written word and carried to the remotest village the message of Loyalist Spain. In the towns it helped create a war atmosphere. With the rebel troops closing in on the city, the spiritual temperature of Madrid rose rapidly when posters were displayed on all her walls calling on the people, with dramatic realism, to resist. When, mirrored in

the posters, the women of Madrid saw themselves attacked by the invaders or separated forever from their children, they rushed to the barricades to finish the work of building and fortification. Every militiaman dreamed of himself as that brave and resolute fighter in whom the artist had symbolized the counterattack which was to save the city. Every workman rebelled against the thought of working under the threat of that Fascist whip which lay outstretched across the poster as though its sinister work had already begun. Some of these posters—in particular those of Renau, a Valencian artist who later held an important position in the Ministry of Education—were quite remarkable. No foreign delegate or writer who visited Republican Spain left the country without taking a set back with him. The finest artists offered their services for this propaganda work, and there was a good deal of friendly rivalry among the various organizations and political parties as to which could produce the best posters (pp. 150–51).

Curiously enough, this competition did not extend to the fascist or Nationalist side. The overwhelming majority of Spanish Civil War posters come from the Republic. Moreover, few of Franco's posters show much artistic invention. The most common fascist posters were images of Franco himself, of which a significant number of different versions were produced. The other common posters on the Nationalist side were produced by the fascist Falangists, generally posters honoring their executed founder and cult figure, José Antonio Primo de Rivera. The Republic also regularly honored individuals—including General Miaja for his leadership in the defense of Madrid—but not repeatedly. The only Loyalist hero to receive a significant number of different poster representations was the anarchist leader Buenaventura Durruti, whom a number of organizations honored after his death in the defense of Madrid, and the Durruti posters themselves show a wild variety of artistic styles. Fascist poster art was thus focused on a cult of personal adulation, which is one reason it is little reproduced or exhibited. As it happens, many of the Franco or Jose Antonio posters reproduce black and white or sepia photographs, which offer little visual impact. Colored borders were not enough to make them graphically powerful. There are perhaps two dozen color fascist posters of some interest—generally heroic battle scenes in a realist style—but they do not add up to a significant component of Spanish Civil War art. A interesting essay about Spanish fascist aesthetics could be written by describing illustrated books, posters, and other visual artifacts, but it would be difficult to sustain an essay based on their posters alone.

There is, however, a substantial amount of Republican art outside the scope of this exhibit that deserves mention, ranging from individual paintings (some of which were exhibited at the Spanish Pavilion in Paris in 1937) to drawings, lithographs, and wood block prints. Some influential Spanish Civil War artists never designed posters, only working in these more traditional media. Others, like Bardasano and Puyol, did both, producing not only posters but also oil paintings, lithographs, magazine and book illustrations, and editorial cartoons. I include examples of Bardasano's prints here to give readers a sense of his stylistic range. Some of their work was mass produced, some of it issued as fine art prints. As other scholars have noted, the scholarship on graphic art of the Spanish Civil War is at an even earlier stage than work on posters. There is no catalogue raisonne of any category of civil war art, but graphic work is not even represented by a book-length selection. Finally, only a few essays deal with Spanish Civil War art from other countries, of which there is a significant amount. We hope this travelling exhibition stimulates funding for some of these projects; indeed, we hope the Abraham Lincoln Brigade Archives is able to help sponsor some of this work.

ARTIST BIOGRAHPIES:
BARDASANO, FONTSERÉ, FRANCISCA, PUYOL, RENAU, SIM

BARDASANO

Born in 1910, the child of Madrid working-class parents, José Bardasano seemed fated for his wartime role from his earliest years. In 1917 his father, a member of the streetcar drivers' strike committee, was jailed when the strike was brutally suppressed. With the father in Modelo prison, the police intimidated Bardasano's mother in her home, precipitating a miscarriage. Meanwhile, Bardasano, age seven, was searched and questioned when he brought a food basket to his father in jail. These were lessons the young boy would not forget. His first education was at a school run by priests, and there too the boy found no pleasure in the exercise of ignorant authority. Already he was drawn to art, making satiric sketches for the other students and skipping school to roam the street in search of itinerant painters. By age ten, Pepito, as he was called, asked permission to join the street painters himself. His father accompanied him, and one Sunday afternoon they were near the monument to Cascorro in the Rastro district in Madrid. A crowd gathered around the young painter and that was enough to attract the attention of the police, who ordered everyone to disperse. The father exhorted the crowd to support them, which they did, and the police decided to withdraw. Another lesson was learned.

José Bardasano

Eventually the father-son team would travel throughout Andalusia, with Bardasano doing quick sketches and selling them in the streets and open markets. In 1921, convinced that he needed formal training, he enrolled in the Arts and Crafts School in Cuatro Caminos. Two years later he received a prize in ornamental drawing, though in 1926 he failed his entrance exams to the Escuela de San Fernando, the main fine arts school in Madrid. He took a job at a company producing ornamental glass doors, but was fired when he sided with striking workers. A job as artistic director of the Rex Advertising Agency followed. Meanwhile, he began to publish his drawings in *El Socialista* and entered a set of prints in the 1932 National Exhibition. Awarded second prize in the same competition two years later, he received a grant from the Count of Cartegena and embarked on a tour of France, Holland, Belgium, and England. In 1936 he received a second travel grant, but refused it when war broke out. Instead he painted *No Pasaran* banners for Madrid streets and entered a public antifascist poster contest held in the immense Plaza Mayor. The winners were chosen by popular ballot, and once again the people in the streets picked Bardasano as their favorite.

Working with three other progressive artists—Alfonso Rodriguez Castelao, Arturo Souto, and Rodríguez Luna—he set up a workshop named *La Gallofa*, which was affiliated with the Plastic Arts section of the JSU (United Socialist Youth Movement). Prints, drawings, and posters came from the workshop in great numbers. Dozens of them were by Bardasano himself; indeed he sent his work to publications throughout Spain. In 1937 he and his wife and brother moved to Valencia, where they continued to produce prints and posters for the JSU Plastic Arts Workshop there. In time his style of expressionist realism became perhaps the signature style of the Spanish Civil War poster. There are other styles, to be sure, from cubist to surrealist to art deco, but Bardasano's is inescapable and omnipresent in the war.

With the war's end, Bardasano struggled to get himself and his family out of Spain. They spent some time in a French concentration camp, but eventually made their way to Mexico. There he formed the Mexican Fine Arts Circle in collaboration with other Spanish exiles and native Mexicans. At first it was the war that dominated his work, and he completed a series of canvases, including *The Retreat*, *Militiawoman*, *Partisan*, and *Terror*. These paintings do not merely memorialize the past; they are blows struck against the repressive regime that then ruled Spain. In time, however, his style broadened. He did a number of formal portraits in a classical academic style to support himself. He also adopted an impressionist canvas to realize his memories of Madrid streets and neighborhoods. In 1957 the Mexican government appointed him its delegate to a Painters and Sculptor's Congress taking place in the Soviet Union. Three years later he decided to return to Spain and settled in Madrid. Eventually, with Franco's death, his country was able to recognize the work done in the crucible of the war. In 1978 his Spanish Civil War posters were again on display in Madrid; the following year, shortly before his death, his work was featured in the exhibit "One Hundred Years of Socialism."

FONTSERÉ

Carles Fontseré was born in 1916 to a petit bourgeois Barcelona family whose members, improbably enough, in the light of Fontseré's adult politics, were loyal Carlists. As anyone familiar with Spanish politics will know, Carlism was an ultra-conservative, ultra-Catholic, monarchist political movement that supported rival claimants to the Spanish throne. Opposed at once to liberalism and to many aspects of modernity, it was a focus of right-wing antagonism toward the Republic from the outset. Indeed, the Carlists organized paramilitary militias in anticipation of the military rising and were important elements of the events of July 18. By that time, of course, Fontseré was on the Left. But some detail about his family's political history is important to keep in mind, because both the family's politics and Fontseré's adolescent identification with them would cause Fontseré himself to fall under suspicion during the war. In fact Fontseré received his name in honor of Don Carlos VII of the Carlists.

By age fourteen Fontseré was already a practicing artist. He usually had a weekly drawing on the first page of *La Protesta* and often did caricatures for *El Correo Catalán*, a bourgeois newspaper. In 1932, at age sixteen, he completed two political posters for the conservative *Dreta de Catalunya* coalition, and two years later did a number of sketches for the right—wing *Front Catalá d'Ordre*. Thereafter, Fontseré gradually drifted away from his family's politics. His own reading helped propel him toward the Left, as did a certain disenchantment with his family. Meanwhile he was frequenting the artist's cafe on Mount Zion street; there he met a number of artists of the Left, including the older Josep Alumá, who was among those who supported him and vouched for him when war broke out.

With the opening of the war Fontseré threw himself into the work of the Syndicate of Professional Artists that had been formed only a few months earlier. The Syndicate requisitioned a large 17th—century mansion on *Avenida de la Puerta del Angel*, at the corner of *Calle Canuda*. Its previous occupants, the Marquises de Barberá and de la Manresana, had been thrown out. Fontseré helped organize a collaborative workshop in the large, well-lit attic, and soon posters were on their way from there to Barcelona's streets.

Later in the war, in 1938, Fontseré would find himself in Albacete, working as an artist for the International Brigades. In the nearby village of Madrigueras, training center at the time for the Garibaldi battalion, he did a large mural of General Miaja in the village Church, along with one in the Cantina and the House of the Soldier. A banner for the car park at Albacete and painted scenery for a play by Rafael Alberti followed. But then Fontseré ran into difficulty. His family's political history was always in the background, establishing a basis for mistrust. When a member of the Teacher's Union in Barcelona denounced him, the chief Political Commissar of the International Brigades, André Marty, detained him and sentenced him to death. As it happened, the sentence was lifted, but it understandably colored Fontseré's perception of the Communist Party's role in the war.

At the very end of the war, near the French border, Fontseré was trying to have a 1939 calendar he had designed printed. But the Republic's time had past. Fontseré fled into France and found himself, like so many refugees, in a concentration camp. French artists managed to secure his freedom, and soon Fontseré was exhibiting drawings of the exodus and the camp in a gallery in Perpignan. When the Second World War broke out he was interned in a concentration camp again, but this time he escaped to Paris. There he managed to survive the war, designing a widely distributed poster to celebrate the city's liberation at the end. After the war he took up painting again, did photography, and designed theater sets for Spanish plays performed in France. Eventually he settled in New York, doing a bit of commercial art and for a time getting by as a taxi driver.

Fontseré returned to Spain in 1973, and, for the next two years did a series of photographic essays for Carlos Sentís's television program Crónica-2; they drew on photographs he had taken over a number of years and included such topics as *A Cab Driver in New York*, *The New America*, *Blacks in Harlem*, *Unusual Mexico*, and *Art in the United States*. On a number of occasions he photographed street people in various cities to chronicle their human geography. After Franco's death, he once again exhibited his work in Barcelona. Indeed, in 1983 an exhibition of his New York photographs, sponsored by the Catalan Generalitat, travelled through the province. The following year saw a Barcelona exhibition of his photographs called *Roma, París, Londres, 1960*.

FRANCISCA

Juana Francisca was born in Madrid in 1914. Even as a child she enjoyed drawing, but like most Spanish women of her generation she was given little opportunity for formal training. As an artist, she was thus largely self-taught. After their marriage in 1934, however, José Bardasano encouraged her to pursue her art, which included both painting and drawing. Thereafter her work was exhibited in Madrid and Paris, but her main focus was illustrating children's books. When the civil war broke out, however, she joined the workshop called *La Gallofa* that Bardasano had organized, and she began to do drawings for wartime informational and propaganda magazines, including *Boletin del Subcomisariado de Propaganda*. Her 1937 drawing *Woman Hugging a Dead Soldier,* executed in pencil and

MAY 1937—CONFERENCE OF THE UNION OF
YOUNG WOMEN OF MADRID

Juana Francisca

watercolor, was exhibited at the Spanish Pavilion in Paris in 1937. Francisca did several posters for the Madrid *Union de Muchachas,* a women's group committed not only to joining the labor force in workshops and factories but also to broadening women's access to cultural and political education, changes she knew to be necessary from her own life experience. Perhaps her single most powerful poster, designed to advertize the May 1937 conference of the Union of Young Women in Madrid, shows three women in a circle holding their arms and hands aloft in the popular front salute. They wear deep brown workers' dresses, and above them their dark yellow blouses and countenances glow with light. It is a striking image of women's political and cultural strength and solidarity.

Since many Spanish Civil War poster artists only signed their work with their last names and a considerable number of posters were issued without an artist's signature, one cannot be certain how many women artists designed posters. However, Juana Francisca's name appears to be the only explicitly female one on wartime posters.

PUYOL

Born in Algeciras (Cádiz) in 1907, Ramón Puyol was trained at the San Fernando Fine Arts School. While still in his teens he was attracted to the avant-garde and exhibited at the First Iberian Artists Show of 1925. By then he was beginning to be known as a graphic illustrator, and his work appeared in such magazines as *La Gaceta Literaria*. He received a grant to work abroad in 1926, and he travelled to Rome and Paris and then England. Returning to Madrid in 1929, he ran the graphics section of the Latin American Publishing House. By then he was doing drawing and painting as well as illustration, and his work appeared in numerous magazines and newspapers, including *La Esfera, Nuevo Mundo, Mundo Gráfico, Estampa,* and *Crónica*.

A CORDOBA. EL CAMPESINADO EN ARMAS!
TO CORDOBA, ITS PEASANTRY IN ARMS
Ramón Puyol

Drawn to politics early in the worldwide depression, he signed the "Manifesto addressed to public opinion and authorities" in 1931, joined the Communist Party, and participated in the First Revolutionary Art Exhibition sponsored by the journal *Octubre* and held in the Madrid Athenaeum in 1933. That same year he designed the theatrical sets for César Falcón's play *Asturias* and travelled to the Soviet Union to work on one of Mayakovsky's theatrical productions. In 1934 he had an individual exhibition at the Madrid Athenaeum and designed the set for Rafael Alberti's *Fermín Galán,* which was produced the following year. *Mundo Obrero*, the Communist Party newspaper, also began publishing his cartoons in 1934.

When war broke out he offered his services to the Republic and did a wide range of different kinds of artistic work, from posters, lithographs, pamphlets, and theater sets to editorial cartoons and illustrations for children's books. He served as editor for the drawing section of César Falcón's group *Altavoz del Frente* (Loudspeaker at the Front), which maintained a large wartime publishing program.

Much of his work, including two oil paintings he exhibited at the Spanish Pavilion in Paris in 1937, falls into the general category of expressionist realism. But he was also attracted to surrealism, and in 1936 he created an extraordinarily inventive series of lithographic portraits that focused surrealist techniques on political caricature. Ten of the lithographs were published as a set by *Altavoz del Frente* in Madrid in February of 1937. Unlike anything else anyone did during the war, they were soon issued as full-scale posters, and Puyol became famous. On a cover sheet Puyol dedicated the folder of prints: "To my brother Miguel, murdered by the fascist horde." Later that year, in a statement of principles prefacing another set of prints, he declared that "the rickety theory of art for art's sake has just died. A class art is born." "The toilers of art," he urged, "should find their aesthetic and even their technique in the concrete trajectory of the workers."[3]

When the war ended, a number of Republican artists fled the country, but Puyol was captured and sentenced to death for his art. Eventually the sentence was commuted to thirty years in prison, but in 1942, when Franco needed someone to restore Tiepolo's frescoes in the monastery of San Lorenzo de Escorial, competent craftsmen were hard to find amongst the fascists. So Puyol was called on, and his sentence was commuted again—this time to six years—in exchange for the work of restoration. Puyol returned to Madrid, but the imaginative fire of the wartime years was either gone or had no outlet. Eventually he settled in the town of his birth, where he died in 1981.

RENAU

Josep (sometime José) Renau was born in Valencia in 1907. His father Josep Renau Montoro was a painter, art restorer, and professor of drawing, so Renau's interest in the arts came

---

[3]   Puyol's text is taken from a Puyol folder at the Humanities Center at the University of Texas at Austin. Full publication information is missing from the copy they obtained at auction.

AL FRONT! (IN CATALAN)

TO THE FRONT! [33 x 23cm]
Carles Fontseré [1936?]. Issued in Barcelona by the CNT/FAI.

ASTURIAS: OCTUBRE, 1934–1937. AYUDA! A LAS FAMILIAS DE LOS COMBATIENTES DEL NORTE

ASTURIAS: OCTOBER, 1934–1937. AID THE FAMILIES OF THE FIGHTERS OF THE NORTH.   [100 x 70CM]
Cheché [1937]. Issued by Spanish Red Aid.

LOS INTERNACIONALES—UNIDOS A LOS ESPAÑOLES, LUCHAMOS CONTRA EL INVASOR

THE INTERNATIONALS—UNITED WITH THE SPANISH WE FIGHT THE INVADER
[100 x 70CM]
Parrilla [1937]. Issued in Madrid by the InternationalBrigades.

EL TRANSPORTE, ES LA LLAVE DE LA SOCIALIZACION Y EL TRIUNFO DE LA REVOLUCION

TRANSPORT IS THE KEY TO SOCIALIZATION AND THE TRIUMPH OF THE REVOLUTION   [100 x 70cm]
Osmundo. Issued by the CNT/FAI/AIT.

EL SOCIALISME ÉS L'ALLIBERACIÓ

SOCIALISM IS LIBERATION   [138 x 99cm]
Anonymous [1936?]. Issued by the POUM.

LA INDUSTRIA L'AGRICULTURA—TOT PER AL FRONT (IN CATALAN)

INDUSTRY, AGRICULTURE—ALL FOR THE FRONT   [33 x 23cm]
Carles Fontseré [1936?]. Issued in Barcelona by the CNT/FAI.

ESPAÑA—CUYAS SEIS LETRAS SONORAS RESTALLAN HOY EN NUESTRA ALMA CON GRITO DE GUERRA Y MAÑANA CON UNA EXCLAMACIÓN DE JÚBILO Y DE PAZ

SPAIN—WHOSE SIX RESOUNDING LETTERS CRACKLE IN OUR SOUL WITH A WAR CRY TODAY AND WITH AN EXCLAMATION OF JOY AND PEACE TOMORROW   [211 x 150cm]
José Bardasano [1937]. Issued in Valencia by the UGT/CNT.

MUJERES TRABAJAR POR LOS COMPAÑEROS QUE LUCHAN

WOMEN, WORK FOR THE COMRADES WHO FIGHT   [100 x 70cm]
Juan Antonio. [Issuing organization unknown]

NUESTROS CAIDOS EXIGEN EL APLASTAMIENTO DE FRANCO

OUR FALLEN DEMAND THAT FRANCO BE CRUSHED   [100 x 70cm]
José Bardasano. Issued by the *Juventudes Socialistas Unificadas* (United Socialist Youth Movement).

UN BORRACHO! ES UN PARÁSITO. ELIMINÉMOSLE!

A DRUNK! HE IS A PARASITE! ELIMINATE HIM! [100 x 70CM]
Artel [1937]. Issued by the Aragon Department of Public Order.

MADRID—7 DE NOVIEMBRE—NO PASARAN!

MADRID—NOVEMBER 7TH—THEY SHALL NOT PASS! [100 x 70CM]
Espert & José Briones [1937]. Issued by Ministry of Propaganda, Madrid Office.

MADRID—CHRETIEN À L'AIDE! ÉCOUTE TA CONSCIENCE ET SAUVE DU MASSACRE MES PETITS ENFANTS D' ESPAGNE

MADRID—CHRISTIANS TO THE RESCUE! LISTEN TO *YOUR CONSCIENCE AND SAVE MY LITTLE CHILDREN OF SPAIN FROM MASSACRE.*   [102 x 72cm]
Pierre Mail.

EL FRUTO DEL TRABAJO DEL LABRADOR ES TAN SAGRADO PARA TODOS COMO EL SALARIO QUE RECIBE EL OBRERO

THE FARMER'S PRODUCE IS AS SACRED AS THE WORKER'S WAGES   [107 x 85cm]
Josep Renau. Issued by the Ministry of Agriculture.

ATENCION! LAS ENFERMEDADES VENERAS AMENAZAN TU SALUD. PREVENTE CONTRA ELLAS!

ATTENTION! VENEREAL DISEASES THREATEN YOUR HEALTH. TAKE STEPS AGAINST THEM. [70 x 48CM]
Rivero Gil. Produced for the army's health ministry.

LOS NACIONALES

THE NATIONALISTS [122 x 97CM]
[Juan Antonio Morales–1936]. Issued by the Ministry of Propaganda.

COLUMNA DE HIERRO—CAMPESINO! LA REVOLUCION TE DARA LA TIERRA

THE IRON COLUMN—PEASANT! THE REVOLUTION GAVE YOU THE LAND   [33 x 23cm]
J. Bauset [1936?]. Issued by the UGT/CNT.

naturally from his family. Indeed, after six years his father took him out of school and made him his assistant. Thus paintings by Velasquez, Goya, Titian, among others, passed through the young boy's hands. Later, as a student at the Fine Arts School in San Carlos, his father's institution, he met a number of other young men and women who would form the core of the Valencian avant-garde. Among them were Antonio Ballester, who also designed posters during the war, and Manuela Ballester, who became Renau's wife.

After completing his studies in 1925 he worked as a painter, assistant to a lithographer, and graphic designer, producing numerous posters, magazine covers, and book jackets. Meanwhile he learned photography, which would prove central to his work thereafter. He moved to Madrid twice, in 1928 and again the following year, but did not feel comfortable there on either trip, returning each time to Valencia. Meanwhile, his paintings and posters were exhibited both in Madrid and in Valencia and sometimes won prizes. In 1932 he took a position as a professor of drawing in the San Carlos School, a position he held until civil war broke out, but it was not the primary source of his inspiration.

That inspiration came from the German expressionist and dadaist movements, from surrealism, and from the various projects fusing art and politics that swept across Europe in the 1920s and 1930s. Renau produced his first photomontage, *The Arctic Man*, in 1929. With the advent of the Second Republic in 1931, experimental European art became increasingly available in Spain, and Renau discovered John Heartfield, George Grosz, and Otto Dix in the German magazine *AIZ*. He also studied the Russian constructivists Rodchenko and Lissitsky carefully and began to apply what he learned in his own work.

Renau also joined the Communist Party in 1931; all this together combined to convince him that art and politics needed to serve one another. Indeed, of all the progressive Spanish artists of his day Renau is unquestionably the most serious and ambitious theorist. Beginning in the 1930s and continuing for the rest of his life, his essays explore a number of issues in political art. He argues, for example, that artists can take possession of the manipulative techniques of advertizing and commercial exploitation, make them self-conscious, turn them against themselves, and make them instruments for the people's liberation. He also reflects on the satisfaction political artists can take in responding to external cultural priorities and needs, rather than their private impulses. In 1934, in the midst of the October revolutionary strike, he was arrested.

With the outbreak of the civil war, Renau became a public figure. He was already the editor of the magazine *Nueva Cultura* and in 1936 became co-director of *Verdad*, the Communist party newspaper in Valencia that made some unifying overtures to the Socialists. That same year the Republican government appointed him Undersecretary for Fine Arts. He was instrumental in appointing Pablo Picasso honorary director of the Prado Museum and in moving the Prado's paintings elsewhere to save them from the Nationalist air raids on Madrid.

Renau, from The American Way of Life

When asked to design the photographic displays for the Spanish Pavilion at the 1937 World's Fair in Paris, he took the job on with great industry. Indeed, he probably made the opening invitation to Picasso to contribute to the Pavilion. Picasso, of course, eventually painted *Guernica*, his single most famous work, and exhibited it there in Paris. Meanwhile, Renau himself was producing some of the war's most memorable posters and photo montages. "The poster-maker," he wrote in 1937, "is the artist of disciplined freedom, of freedom conditioned by objective exigencies, that is to say, external to his individual will." His final wartime project was a series of thirteen montages titled *The Thirteen Points of Negrín*, designed to illustrate the prime minister's plan for winning the war.

With the war's end Renau escaped to France and made his way to Mexico. There he collaborated with the Mexican painter and Spanish Civil War veteran David Siqueiros on a large mural for the Electrician's union. But it would be photomontage that would occupy him most deeply for the rest of his life. Given his proximity to the most powerful capitalist nation on earth, and given his interest in transforming and undermining commercial imagery, it is perhaps not surprising that he turned toward the United States and its popular iconography. The idea for a comprehensive satiric and critical photo montage of American consumerism and political ideology gradually took hold in him. He collected and categorized a vast quantity of illustrations from magazines like *Life* and *Fortune* and began cutting and assembling them in dramatic color collages.

The project took more than twenty years to complete. Meanwhile, in 1958 he left Mexico for East Germany. According to East German writers, he left because the C.I.A. was plotting an attempt on his life. A selection from his collage series, *Fata Morgana—The American Way of Life*, was published in 1967 and the entire series of 69 images was finally issued in 1989. It explodes and ridicules American notions of gender, parodies and exaggerates the culture of consumerism, and indicts American racism with special force. But it also takes up specific topics, from the Korean war to the Klu Klux Klan to American popular culture. It is paralleled by another Renau collage series, *Über Deutschland*, that takes the Federal Republic of Germany as its object.

Renau made his first return trip to Spain in 1976, the year after Franco died, ending thirty—seven years of exile and exhibiting his work in his homeland for the first time since the civil war. In 1978 the Catalan writer Joan Fuster wrote an open letter to him: "All your life you have been an artist for the street: placards, posters, photomontages . . . You really aren't a `painter.' You are a fighter whose weapons are the instruments of painters." Renau's collected essays were soon published in Spain, and he established a foundation in his name. He died in 1982.

SIM

When the army rebelled against the elected government of Spain in July 1936 it was largely ordinary people, not any preexisting military force, who kept the generals from success. All over Spain informal people's militias had sprung up to defend their Republic against the military uprising. They broke into military barracks and armed themselves, and in the mountain passes north of Madrid and in the bullet-torn streets of Barcelona, they put down the military rebellion and gave their country free ground to hold. There was a young artist, born in the twentieth century's first decade, who took up the name "Sim" and travelled with those militias in the summer and fall of 1936 to document their story. He took with him linen paper, India ink, and a box of watercolors to chronicle the men and women of the militias in battle and at rest. With his sketches, in particular, of women brandishing rifles from commandeered trucks or moving across a field of battle with pistol in hand, Sim could not help but catch the world's attention. And he did. *Estampas de la Revolucion Española 19 Julio de 1936—*

YOUTH—A political upheaval upset her girlish games and pastimes. With interest she surveyed the heroic struggle that was played before her eyes, the struggle of a people for life and liberty. Drawn to the combat by the general enthusiasm, she joined the fighters and handles the rifle with a joy and a fervor that bodes well for the Social Revolution.

Sim

a spiral-bound book of reproductions with captions in Spanish, French, and English—became the most widely known art of the Spanish Civil War until Picasso unveiled his wartime masterpiece, *Guernica*, in the fall of 1937.

Sim's 1936 sketches were done in a distinctive style—quick, angular black brush strokes overlaid with swaths of diluted primary reds, blues, greens, and yellows. No one else would imitate this style during the war; it became his signature. Sim was actually the pen name of Rey Vila, a small, thin, blonde, blue-eyed young man who had studied at the School of Fine Arts in Barcelona and was then radicalized by military service in Africa. In fact he was with the Spanish army in Morocco at the time of the distaster at Anual, on July 21, 1921, when general Fernandez Silvestre and a force of 20,000 Spaniards were lured beyond their supply lines and defeated by the Riffians under Abd-el-Krim; 12,000 Spanish troops died in the battle, and it suggested to Vila at once the futility of military occupation and the nightmarish nature of war. So his chronicle of the heady first months of the Spanish Civil War was not done in romantic naivite. As the editors of Sim's 1937 portfolio *12 Escenas de Guerra* put it in their introduction, "he had experienced the terrible effects produced by shameless politicians and mercenaries on the affairs of State, and as a result had become a stout defender of the people. This is why his sketches have so impulsive a style."

Sim's 1936 sketches are dominated by the red and black colors of the FAI, the group of theoreticians and activists who made up the ideological vanguard of Spanish anarchism. Sim's pseudonym, too, amounts to a flamboyant gesture of anonymity, comparable to the many anarchist artists and writers who issued their work unsigned. *Estampas* was followed by a new portfolio of drawings, *12 Escenas de Guerra*, in much more muted colors, and by a series of Sim reproductions and transpositions in multiple forms—wartime calendars for 1937 and 1938, postcards, and full-sized posters that became equally widely known. He did a number of posters for the "week of the children" in 1937. Taken together, Sim's sketches constitute what Carles Fontseré has called an "iconography of the revolution," the people's spontaneous resistance to the military coup. With individual portraits and group scenes of men and women in battle, marching through streets among celebratory flags, tending to the wounded, aiding comrades under fire, Sim's art captures the egalitarian spirit of the people's armed resistance to fascism. Distributed abroad, his work left behind its local political context to become an international symbol of solidarity and resistance. Indeed *Estampas* was widely distributed in the United States and in Europe.

After the war, Sim eventually made his way to Paris, where his studio in the Buttes Chaumont, shared with numerous pet doves, was home both to his series of bullfight paintings and to his numerous illustrations for *Don Quixote*. Indeed, decades after the civil war was over,

diners in Spanish restaurants in various cities across the world might well have noticed reproductions of bullfight paintings done with angular black brush strokes overlaid with swaths of primary colors. If some of those diners were veterans of the Spanish Civil War, as they may well have been, they may have felt more than a twinge of recognition as matadors and bulls stared one another down over the dinner table. For once upon a time—when the world was occupied with the first great battles of what would become the apocalyptic confrontation between fascism and democracy—sketches in exactly that style had travelled the world to introduce everyone to the remarkable events taking place on the Iberian Peninsula. These postwar bullfight paintings, however, were not signed with the name "Sim" but rather "Rey Vila," a name generally unknown during the war.

THE GOSSIP *IS A COMPANION PIECE TO HIS* EL RUMOR
[AUTHORS COLLECTION]
Ramón Puyol [1936]

NUMBER 1

José Bardasano [1937]

SHOUTS FROM THE WALL: AN ANNOTATED GUIDE TO THE EXHIBIT

ORGANIZATIONAL RATIONALE

The exhibit is organized into four major sections. The first section—emphasizing the struggle between democracy and fascism and including several anti-war images of civilians suffering history's first saturation bombing of civilian targets—covers the broad international issues that were most relevant at the time and remain most accessible now. The second section introduces people to four major poster artists with four very different artistic styles, from Sim's rapidly executed sketches in India ink and water color wash to Puyol's astonishing surrealist portraits. The third section deals with the variety of political and social issues that both the Spanish government and political groups used color posters to discuss and promote, from aid to the Basques in the north to the cost of alcoholism. Finally, a Lincoln Brigade album gives viewers the more personal story of the Americans in Spain. Appropriate wall text and photographs occur throughout the exhibit.

PART ONE: *THE STRUGGLE AGAINST FASCISM*

Picture yourself one moonlit night in Madrid late in 1936. Visibility is good, so the fascist bombers are out in force. Germany's Adolph Hitler has provided his Condor Legion to help General Francisco Franco bomb his own capital city into submission. As the residents of Barcelona would also come to learn in the course of the war, five hundred pound bombs are a serious weapon; they burrow deep into a building before exploding. Meanwhile, at the city's edge, high on Mount Garabitas above the wooded hills of the Casa de Campo, Franco's soldiers have set the sights of their artillery pieces on the city's landmarks. The Telephonica building gives them a range finder and a line of sight.

When the air raid siren sounds you seek out the nearby subway *refugio*. There, as people gather together amidst repeated detonations, powerless, unable to strike back, the bright colors of the posters on the subway walls remind you that elsewhere your comrades are striking back. And they remind you that the city's anguish is at once exemplary and exceptional, that it is the object of the world's attention. Later, when the sun rises over smoking ruins, it brightens the bold colors of resistance and solidarity on posters covering walls still standing.

Madrid is of one mind; these posters are its hues and its icons, the forms in which it knows itself. These are some of the posters that helped strengthen the Spanish people's resolve. Here are the posters that helped waken the world to the nature of the conflict in Spain.

1. ESPAÑA—CUYAS SEIS LETRAS SONORAS RESTALLAN HOY EN NUESTRA ALMA CON GRITO DE GUERRA Y MAÑANA CON UNA EXCLAMACIÓN DE JÚBILO Y DE PAZ
SPAIN——WHOSE SIX RESOUNDING LETTERS CRACKLE IN OUR SOUL WITH A WAR CRY TODAY AND WITH AN EXCLAMATION OF JOY AND PEACE TOMORROW [211 x 150CM]
José Bardasano [1937]. Issued in Valencia by the UGT/CNT.

NUMBER 2
Parilla [1937]

NUMBER 3
Anonymous [1937]

NUMBER 4
Pierre Mail [1937]

The Unión General de Trabajodores (UGT) was Spain's powerful socialist trade union, the *Confederación Nacional del Trabajo* (CNT) its powerful anarcho– syndicalist union. Each had about a million members.

The imposing lion in this poster, nearly seven feet tall, stands in front of the red, yellow, and purple flag of the Spanish Republic. The lion's right foot is crushing a fasces, the bundle of rods with an ax blade facing out that symbolized Italian fascism. With a distinctly humanized face, the lion represents not only the country and people of Spain but also their capital city, Madrid. In fact the Republic used a lion in posters issued before the war began. Though not the standard symbol for the city, the lion is closely associated with Madrid's public architecture. In the *Plaza de la Cibeles*, before the Palace of Communications, stands the great fountain and statue representing the Greek goddess Cybele, honored as the mother of all life and mistress of the animals. Following traditional iconography, her chariot is pulled by two immense stone lions. During the Spanish Civil war the statue was sandbagged to protect it from fascist bombs. Elsewhere in Madrid, the Congress of Deputies is flanked by two bronze lions made from cannons melted down after they were captured from the Moors during the African war in the 19th century. Finally, four stone lions overlook the pond in Madrid's Retiro park.

2. GENERAL MIAJA—EL PUEBLO DE MADRID A SU HEROICO DEFENSOR
GENERAL MIAJA—THE PEOPLE OF MADRID TO THEIR HEROIC DEFENDER   [100 x 70cm]
Parrilla [1937]. Issued by the Madrid Defense Committee.

This poster gives tribute to General José Miaja, head of the Madrid Defense Committee formed when the government abandoned the capital in November 1936; Miaja's portrait is on the left. The Madrid statue to the Greek goddess Cybele is pictured below. The woman's profile to Miaja's right probably evokes both the goddess Cybele and *La Niña Bonita* (the beautiful maiden), symbol of the Second Spanish Republic. The placement of the two profiles makes a symbolic couple of Miaja and *La Niña Bonita*.

3. MADRID—QUE FAIS-TU POUR EMPECHER CELA?
MADRID—WHAT ARE YOU DOING TO STOP THIS?   [80 x 56cm]
Anonymous [1937]. Issued in Madrid by the Ministry of Propaganda.

This poster was printed in Spain in Spanish, English, and French versions for international distribution. The angular arrangement of its various elements recalls the heyday of Soviet experimental poster art in the 1920s.

4. MADRID—CHRETIEN À L'AIDE! ÉCOUTE TA CONSCIENCE ET SAUVE DU MASSACRE MES PETITS ENFANTS D'ESPAGNE
MADRID—CHRISTIANS TO THE RESCUE! LISTEN TO YOUR CONSCIENCE AND SAVE MY LITTLE CHILDREN OF SPAIN FROM MASSACRE.   [102 x 72cm]
Pierre Mail.

NUMBER 5

Anonymous [c. 1937]

NUMBER 6

Ras [1936]

NUMBER 7

Muro

42

This is one of several posters by French artist Pierre Mail, printed in France as part of the international artistic response to the war.

5. AYUDA A MADRID—LA AVIACIÓN FASCISTA PASA SOBRE LA CAPITAL DE LA REPÚBLICA. HACES TÚ ALGO PARA EVITAR ESTO?

AID MADRID—THE FASCIST AIR FORCE IS FLYING OVER THE CAPITAL OF THE REPUBLIC. WHAT ARE YOU DOING TO PREVENT THIS? [91 x 65cm]
Anonymous [c. 1937]. Issued by the Council for the Defense of Madrid.

A photographic poster showing two children seeking refuge under a bridge or culvert from an air attack.

6. CRIMINALES!

CRIMINALS! [100 x 70cm]
Ras [1936]. Issued in both English and Spanish by the POUM's Red Aid.

The POUM *(Partido Obrero de Unificación Marxista)* was a revolutionary Marxist party that was hostile to the leadership of the Soviet Union. The POUM's main strength was in Catalonia and its capital Barcelona. The POUM's Red Aid was its alternative to International Red Aid, organized by the Comintern. The organization promoted political awareness and helped in social welfare projects. This image of an anguished mother carrying her dead child, virtually offering to hand the body to the viewer, may have influenced Picasso's *Guernica*.

7. KULTUR!—LA BARBARIE FASCISTE A MADRID

CULTURE! FASCIST BARBARITY IN MADRID [100 x 70cm]
Muro. Issued in Valencia by the CNT/AIT.

The AIT or *Asoción Internacional de Trabajadores* (International Working Men's Association) was was the Spanish branch of the International Association of Anarcho-Syndicalist workers. It was formed in competition with the communist and socialist Internationals.

"Kultur!" is in German in all versions of the poster, suggesting that this is how the culture of German fascism and its air force expresses itself in Madrid. The rest of the text is in Dutch, French, or Spanish, in alternate versions of the poster. Eleven numbered photographs of bombing damage, arranged to form a swastika, are identified in a key below: 1) Opera Square with the Opera Cinema and some houses after bombardment; 2) The bombs of factionists are used mainly against innocent children; here a poor baby lies beside other corpses killed by aerial machine–gun fire; 3) Here is what remains of the flaming Church of Saint Sebastian on Atocha Street after aerial bombardment by "nationalists" who call themselves "defenders of the Church"!; 4) The popular Globe Pharmacy on Anton Martin Street, demolished by barbarous aerial bombardment; 5) Once more, babies with their inoffensive parents at the depositing place for corpses; 6) Another view of Mayor Street, with the Cinema Pleyel; 7) Houses demolished by bombs of the pirates of the air; 8) Another view of the Globe pharmacy with Atocha Street to the right; 9) The effects of aerial bombardment of Alcala Street at the corner of

NUMBER 8

Espert & José Briones [1937]

NUMBER 9

Pere Catalá Roca [1936]

the Puerta del Sol; 10) The fascist brutes do not take age into account; for them, it is a matter of killing people, even children!; 11) Detail of the market on Carmen Street, demolished by aerial bombs.

8. MADRID—7 DE NOVIEMBRE—NO PASARAN!

MADRID—NOVEMBER 7TH—THEY SHALL NOT PASS!   [100 x 70CM]
Espert & José Briones [1937]. Issued by Ministry of Propaganda, Madrid Office.

Issued to honor the people's defense of Madrid; its dominant blue color may evoke the blue overalls that were standard worker's attire. On November 7th, 1936, the Madrid Defense Committee took over the city. General Francisco Franco, head of the military rebellion, announced that the city would fall the next day; instead Madrid resisted his armies for over two years. *No Pasaran!* was the slogan that echoed worldwide to symbolize the people's determination that Franco would not capture the capital. At the center of the poster is a little collage of images of some of the city's famous public architecture. The *telefonica* building, located at the city's high point, was a frequent target of fascist artillery; it is uppermost in the collage. In the center are the multiple arches of the *Puerta de Alcalá*. To the left, atop a dome, is a winged figure that rises above a building at the juncture of *Calle de Alcalá* and the *Gran Via*. The poster shows evidence of the expressionist influence on Spanish Civil War art.

9. AIXAFEM FEIXISME (IN CATALAN)

SMASH FASCISM   [100 x 70CM]
Pere Catalá Roca [1936]. Issued by the Commissariat of Propaganda, Government of Catalonia.

A photomontage of a sandaled foot crushing a swastika on a dampened cobbled street. The rope-soled sandals, *alpargatas*, are traditional peasant footwear, suggesting that it is the common people who will crush the fascist invaders. Note that the swastika was reversed when the montage was made. Australian surrealist poet Mary Low mentions seeing the poster after an evening at the theater in Barcelona in 1936. The passage occurs toward the end of *Red Spanish Notebook*, the memoir she coauthored with Cuban revolutionary Juan Brea: "We stood outside the columned portico, in front of us a poster flapped in the rain—a foot in a Catalan sandal crushing a swastika with negligent, unquestioned strength" (p.226)

NUMBER 10

SHE SAW HIM FALL—When her chum fell, riddled by the enemy's lead, she saw his eyes glaze in death, then seizing the rifle from the stiffening hands she stood proudly erect and shouted: I shall avenge you.

Sim [1936]

NUMBER 10

DELIRIUM—A wounded soldier in delirium, horrible visions torture him, wearing down his energy and resistance. For the hundreth time he tries to rise. The hospital nurse is at his side, tender as a mother, loving as a sister; she does all that is possible to soothe his pain.

Sim [1936]

PART TWO: FOUR ARTISTS

SIM, BARDASANO, PUYOL, RENAU

Four poster artists of the Spanish Civil War. Four styles, four visions of Spain's agony and her utopian future.

With Sim, the name Rey Vila adopted for his civil war posters and prints, the present struggle—despite all its carnage—nonetheless gives us glimpses of a future based on class solidarity and gender equality. It is a future whose heroes embody general needs and aspirations rather than personal ones. As we see from his images of women at war, it is a future in which the differences between men and women carry no prejudicial social meaning. That this future is possible, realizable, is evident as much as anything in the confidence of Sim's brush strokes.

With José Bardasano too a vision of the future is implied in the way his soldiers handle the challenges of the present. The justice of their cause is absolute, and they pursue it with all their being. When they fight, every muscle lends itself to the battle. When they die, the near world reddens with their blood. Bardasano's expressionist realism means that all his images are given an extra intensity, that his draughtsmanship seeks out not only form but value.

With Ramón Puyol, a political satire at once caustic and whimsical takes over. He also did paintings in an expressionist realist style, but his most famous works are no doubt the more than forty partly surrealist portraits he produced in Madrid, about ten of which were issued as posters. His portraits, simultaneously grotesque and playful, leave us uncertain whether we should be charmed or scandalized. But the figurative wit is never separable from social and political critique. Puyol's is a rogue's gallery of ordinary, everyday villains, class types who exaggerate every feature of their social positioning.

Finally, at his best, Josep Renau, based in Valencia, always seeks an unforgettable image to embody his moral and political claims on us. From now on the thought of ultimate victory may be inseparable from the enraptured aviator who gazes at the sweep of planes above him. Any unreasonable seizure of land is linked to the thought of that grasping, bayonetted hand as it seeks a farmer's property.

10. WOMEN AT WAR—BY SIM [1936].
"YOUTH," "THEY SHALL NOT PASS," "SHE KNEW HOW TO DIE," "SHE SAW HIM FALL," "BATTERING RAM," "REST," "AFTER THE STRUGGLE," "DELERIUM." [27 x 35CM (HORIZONTAL) 35 x 27CM (VERTICAL)]

The Spanish Civil War accelerated a radical transformation in the status of women in the Republic. Women took up work in the factories; they had wide access to education for the first time; their legal status was secured; women's organizations and cultural journals were founded; abortion was legalized; and, most surprisingly from the viewpoint of the rest of the world, women fought in the front lines in the opening months of the war. The captions printed beneath Sim's prints were published with the prints in three languages—Spanish, French, and English. The red and black colors of anarchism dominate a number of the prints in the series.

NUMBER 11

José Bardasano

NUMBER 12

José Bardasano

NUMBER 13

José Bardasano [1937]

Sim's images of armed women striding forward purposefully in battle are still striking and unconventional, even after sixty years. But the series of prints actually plays havoc with gender stereotypes in a variety of ways. The captions to *Battering Ram* and *Rest* are gender neutral, and the prints depict men and women as equals. The captions to *She Saw Him Fall* and *She Knew How to Die* substitute female pronouns in rhetoric more familiar from paeans to male heroism and resolve and thus demolish the notion that these traits are gender specific. The captions to *Youth* and *They Shall Not Pass,* on the other hand, are partly inflected to account for their gendered subject. Most conventional of all, of course, is *Delirium*, which shows a nurse ministering to a feverish soldier. But there are several prints in the series devoted to the medical services, and one, *In the Thick of the Fight,* shows a militiaman and a nurse carrying a wounded figure from a battle in progress; the gender neutral caption describes them both as "symbols of the revolution . . . muscles taut and a spark of rebelliousness in their hearts." Of the thirty–one prints in the series (plus one on the cover), all executed in 1936 and not all depicting people, fifteen of them have women as their sole or equal subject. Sim's *Estampas de la Revolución Española 19 Julio de 1936* was published in Barcelona by the propaganda offices of the CNT/FAI.

By the spring of 1937 images of women in battle essentially disappeared from Republican posters and graphic art. By then the militias had largely been absorbed into the new more conventional army.

11. NUESTROS CAIDOS EXIGEN EL APLASTAMIENTO DE FRANCO
OUR FALLEN DEMAND THAT FRANCO BE CRUSHED   [100 x 70CM]
José Bardasano. Issued by the *Juventudes Socialistas Unificadas* (United Socialist Youth Movement).

The three Bardasano posters in sequence here are excellent examples of the style of expressionist realism that characterized most of his wartime art and of which he was perhaps the master among the Republic's poster artists. The deep orange red of the first poster makes not only the body but also the ground on which it lies seem massively wounded, while the halo of white light framing the fallen soldier makes his wounded valor explosively radiant.

12. TREBALLADORS! EL FEIXISME ES L'EXPLOTACIO I L'EXCLAVATGE. 100,000 VOLUNTARIS. (IN CATALAN)
WORKERS! FASCISM IS EXPLOITATION AND SLAVERY. 100,000 VOLUNTEERS NEEDED.   [109 x 73CM]
José Bardasano. Issued by the Popular Front of Catalonia.

A worker is crucified against a swastika. As with Bardasano's other posters, this iconography amounts to symbolism with many perfectly realist analogues.

13. 18 DE JULIO, 1936–1937
THE EIGHTEENTH OF JULY, 1936 TO 1937   [100 x 68CM]
José Bardasano [1937]. [Issuing organization unknown]

The military rebellion began on July 18, 1936, and so did the people's defense of their country. This poster commemorates a year of resistance to fascism. Its graphic depiction of hand- to-hand combat,

NUMBER 14

Ramón Puyol [1936–37]

in which a Republican soldier wearing a Spanish helmet grapples with a Nazi, reduces the struggle to its most basic element. The German carries a stick grenade on his belt, and he reaches up with his clawed hand to grasp his enemy, but none of this is to any avail. The Republican soldier strides forward in a confident, sweeping posture that crushes Hitler's agent against the barbed wire of one of his concentration camps.

14. EL RUMOR—GUERRA A MUERTE AL RUMOR! QUE INTENTA DESTROZAR NUESTRA MORAL Y NUESTRA UNIÓN

RUMOR—WAR TO THE DEATH ON RUMOR, WHOSE PURPOSE IS TO DESTROY OUR MORALE AND UNITY!
[88 x 64CM]
Ramón Puyol [1936– 37]. Issued by *Socorro Rojo Internacional* (International Red Aid).

International Red Aid was organized by the Comintern in 1921 to promote the economic liberation of the working classes. During the Spanish Civil War SRI became involved in charitable fund-raising for a number of social welfare functions. With its assistance to front-line hospitals it became the equivalent of the Spanish Red Cross. Puyol's 1936 lithographs were most likely not issued as posters until 1937.

A set of ten lithograph versions of Puyol's surrealist portraits was issued for sale at the Spanish Pavilion at the Paris Exposition of 1937. In that version of *El Rumor* the winged figure is dramatically hermaphroditic, a kind of somatic version of the multiplication of stories and identities: a prominent erect penis protrudes from a vagina. When a smaller version of the poster was reproduced in a wartime selection of prints by several artists, *Los Dibujantes en la Guerra de España*, the editors rather clumsily removed El Rumor's penis, but left the vagina intact, no doubt unintentionally producing a female version of the print. The large, multiply– sexed lithograph version was designed for private purchase, rather than public display in Spain. When *Socorro Rojo Internacional* wanted to publish *El Rumor* as a poster, Puyol redesigned it to be sexually neutral; the poster has a smooth, unsexed, featureless line where the genitals once were. Despite widespread anti-clericism in the Republic, Spain was still culturally a conservative Catholic country; public display of a penis or a vagina was deemed unacceptable.

It is worth noting that the motif of multiple lips occurs earlier in Spanish surrealism, though Puyol's overall figure is very much his own invention. Published as part of the campaign against fifth columnists, the poster warns of the dangers of loose talk. Here "rumor" is all lips but no ears, manufacturing rumors and broadcasting them everywhere. (With four military columns heading toward Madrid, the fascists boasted that a fifth column of sympathizers would rise up from within the capital to help them capture the city.) Even *El Rumor's* eyes have been replaced by lips, a particularly uncanny device because the lips double as eyelids. Nigel Glendinning remarks that "the winged feet and shoulders are harder to explain. Presumably, they are meant to convey the rapidity with which rumors travel as well as their ubiquity. Might they also be parody versions of Cupid (son of the God of War) and Mercury (the God of Lying)?" The floating rectangular shapes projected from the figure's lips may be coffins, suggesting the deadly power of rumor in wartime.

NUMBER 15

Ramón Puyol [1936– 37]

NUMBER 16

Ramón Puyol [1936– 37]

It should be noted that the danger inherent in wartime rumors in Spain was considerable. Remember, for example, that some foreign papers printed headlines in 1936 anticipating the imminent fall of Madrid. When rumors seemed credible, morale could be seriously undermined. The fascist radio stations took advantage of people's volatile emotions and broadcast false rumors continuously. So the object of Puyol's attack is by no means trivial.

15. EL ESPIA—SILENCIO! EL ENEMIGO ACECHA EN TODAS PARTES.
SPY —SILENCE! THE ENEMY LIES IN WAIT EVERYWHERE.   [88 x 64CM]
Ramón Puyol [1936– 37]. Issued by SRI.

The spy has been grotesquely adapted to his surveillance function, with huge protruding eyes and ears and a body that incorporates the technology of his trade, notably a radio antenna springing from his head. A cross above his nearly toothless mouth suggests he may sometimes assume a pastoral disguise, but his long clawed and spidery hands and half-rotted clothes make his ghoulish nature clear. A March 16, 1937, article in the newspaper *ABC* observed that "in Puyol there is something very Spanish, and this is a taste for symbols, allegories, emblems, moralities."

16. EL IZQUIERDISTA—EL EMBOSCADO SE CUBRE DE TODOS LOS ROPAJES PARA MEJOR ASESINAR EN LA SOMBRA! ANIQUILÉMOSLE SE ENCUENTRE DONDE SE ENCUENTRE!
THE ULTRALEFTIST—THE AMBUSHER WEARS MANY DISGUISES TO ASSASINATE FROM UNDER COVER! WE ANNIHILATE HIM WHEREVER WE FIND HIM!   [88 x 64CM]
Ramón Puyol [1936– 37]. Issued by SRI.

This poster takes its visual style from surrealism but its thematics from the conflicted world of Spanish politics. Both the Left and the Right in Spain were made up of multiple parties with competing aims and social visions. The communist party, following its worldwide popular front policy, argued for cooperation with liberal democrats and socialists in the struggle against fascism. The more radical Left, on the other hand, promoted continuing class struggle and a continuing social revolution. This poster presents the communist party view of the radical Left, mainly anarchists and the POUM. The "ultraleftist" here, at once absurd and grotesque, overdoes everything. He raises two right hands in the closed– fist salute of the Popular Front and wears not the one conventional five-pointed star of the people's army but two, along with the three stripes of the Republic's flag on his sleeve. His nose, elongated Pinocchio-style, is stretched out in yet a third Popular Front fist. His left foot, meanwhile, has melded with a tree trunk; stuck in the ground, he can neither move nor adapt. And his right leg, clothed in shredded striped trousers, suggests he is imprisoned in old ideas. He wears a Soviet hammer and sickle proudly on his chest, but his real identity, hidden away inside him, is here exposed for all to see: in place of his heart sits a fat capitalist in a top hat. Behind his head, therefore, we see that the Left and the Right hands are really clasped together in collaboration. Finally, the tree trunk is sprouting an arm that offers the open-handed fascist salute. It is really

NUMBER 17

Josep Renau

NUMBER 18

Josep Renau [1938]

fascism, the poster argues, that ultimately benefits from the divisive policies of the radical Left. Those politics, the ultraleftist's pointed ears suggest, have a demonic or bestial character.

17. EL FRUTO DEL TRABAJO DEL LABRADOR ES TAN SAGRADO PARA TODOS COMO EL SALARIO QUE RECIBE EL OBRERO

THE FARMER'S PRODUCE IS AS SACRED AS THE WORKER'S WAGES   [107 x 85CM]
Josep Renau. Issued by the Ministry of Agriculture.

This poster probably argues against too rapid collectivization of agriculture; that may be the import of warning us that a farmer's produce belongs to him much as a worker's wages does. The poster thus defends a peasant's individual right to his land. The Ministry of Agriculture, headed by the communist Vicente Uribe, seized land belonging to Nationalists and gave it to collectives but resisted efforts to seize large Republican properties.

18. VICTORIA—HOY MAS QUE NUNCA

VICTORY—TODAY MORE THAN EVER   [100 x 136CM]
Josep Renau [1938]. Issued by the Subsecretariat of Propaganda.

Renau's *Victory* poster, issued in 1938, may well commemorate the brief moment that spring when France opened its borders to allow the Republic to be partially resupplied with planes and other material. Note the planes that make up the poster's "V." Renau was also an experimental photographer and was particularly interested in photomontage. These influences are evident in the magic realist, almost solarized appearance of the aviator at the poster's lower left. Renau's success here at integrating the text and the graphic image is not unique among Spanish Civil War posters but it is relatively uncommon.

NUMBER 19

Anonymous [1936?]

PART THREE: ART AND POLITICS

Imagine walking through various quarters in Madrid or Barcelona in 1936 or 1937. These are wartime cities devoted to an ongoing (and absolutely necessary) form of public discussion and debate. No one ignores the public sphere, for its fate will shape any possibility for a private life thereafter. The detailed arguments about how to pursue the war and the social changes desired by so many of the people have raged in cafes and newspapers and open plazas for months. Now they can be summoned in a phrase, and those phrases are to be found vibrantly illustrated on posters placed on walls throughout the city. These posters are icons of political debate and critical public information. They encapsulate philosophies in a phrase, personify whole populations in a single figure. They amount to a graphic staging of the imagery and discourses of political and cultural life in Spain. And it is their very diversity that sustains the plurality of points of view in the population. From time to time a single theme or issue takes over the walls and focuses everyone's attention on it, but over the months and often in a single long walk through various neighborhoods the posters stage all the controversies and imperatives of public life.

We present here a representative anthology of the topics and viewpoints taken up in wartime posters in the Spanish Republic. Multiply their numbers, add music and explosions and a sense that the future of the world is at stake, and they can take you back to that imperiled moment when World War II was about to begin, but when it still seemed that it might be prevented.

19. EL SOCIALISME ÉS L'ALLIBERACIÓ

SOCIALISM IS LIBERATION   [138 x 99cm]
Anonymous [1936?]. Issued by the POUM.

Designed anonymously, perhaps as early as 1936, for the POUM *(Partido Obrero de Unificación Marxista)*, a revolutionary Marxist party that was hostile to the leadership of the Soviet Union. The caption has several connotations. First, it is a general affirmation of socialism, something about which several Spanish political parties would have agreed. Second, it suggests the POUM is socialism's true incarnation, a point very much in dispute. Third, it makes a statement about socialism, that it is devoted to the revolutionary liberation of ordinary working people, a group of whom gazes upward and fills most of the poster. Throughout the war the Spanish Left argued about whether winning the war or promoting progressive social change should be their primary focus. This poster argues for the latter position, rejecting military regimentation or cooperation with the central government as primary goals. The poster also uses clothing to make its point. Note that, although several of the men wear blue worker's caps, two of the figures in the center wear the peaked brown cap of the militias. The soldier, so the poster argues, should not be part of an independent force but rather an inextricable member of the common people and an expression of their collective identity. Although it is often argued that 1930s political art presents working–class people as anonymous, monumentalized figures, here is an effort to depict working people as recognizable individuals, not merely as symbols; yet they are also clearly unified by revolutionary aspiration.

NUMBER 20

Carles Fontseré [1936?]

NUMBER 21

Carles Fontseré [1936?]

NUMBER 22

J. Bauset [1936?]

20. AL FRONT! (IN CATALAN)

TO THE FRONT!   [33 x 23CM]
Carles Fontseré [1936?]. Issued in Barcelona by the CNT/FAI.

The FAI or *Federación Anarquista Ibérica* was the ideological vanguard of Spanish anarchism.

Fontsere's soldier wears a Spanish helmet of 1926 design. This is one of a number of posters issued in both large and small formats. It was probably part of the early mobilization efforts. The extreme contrast between light and shadow make this soldier an emotionally powerful icon. The burst of light on his helmet helps make him a positive, rather than forbidding, image.

21. LA INDUSTRIA L'AGRICULTURA—TOT PER AL FRONT (IN CATALAN)

INDUSTRY, AGRICULTURE—ALL FOR THE FRONT   [33 x 23CM]
Carles Fontseré [1936?]. Issued in Barcelona by the CNT/FAI.

Often in conflict, industry and agriculture, or so the poster suggests, are united by the crisis produced by the war.

22. COLUMNA DE HIERRO—CAMPESINO! LA REVOLUCION TE DARA LA TIERRA

THE IRON COLUMN—PEASANT! THE REVOLUTION GAVE YOU THE LAND   [33 x 23CM]
J. Bauset [1936?]. Issued by the UGT/CNT.

The Iron Column, or Iron Battalion, made up in part of former prisoners from Valencia, served under officers from the anarchosyndicalist CNT trade union in the first eight months of the war. As a militia unit, it operated independently until it was forcibly integrated into the regular army in March 1937. No other column had displayed a more fierce antagonism toward the centralized state; it was thus a signal representative of one version of anarchism. In the opening months of the war it was noted for attacks on land owners and members of the middle classes. The slogan on the right urges people to recognize that it was the social and political revolution following the military rising, not any action of the government, that broke up the large estates and gave land to Spain's peasants.

For a graphic representation of conflicts among the various parties of the Spanish Left, compare this poster with number 16, Puyol's *El Izquierdista*. They are essentially two views of the same figure. Puyol shows the communist party's view of Spain's anarchist and radical Marxist Left; in his poster the capitalist is *inside* the anarchist. Here, in Bauset's poster, the raging capitalist monster is an external enemy, kept impaled on a bayonet by the anarchist soldier who stands astride Spain as its only defender. So Bauset shows the anarchist as a hero, while Puyol showed him as compromised by (thus aiding) the very enemy he was supposed to resist. Note that the soldier in Bauset's portrait has a leather ammunition box on his belt but is otherwise without a uniform. Indeed, he is bare-chested, to suggest it is his natural state to resist fascism. The porcine capitalist is wearing a stole that has the yoke and arrows (symbol of the right-wing Falange party) at its end. It almost seems he is being flung over the soldier's shoulder like a bale of hay.

NUMBER 23

J. Bauset [1936?]

NUMBER 24

M. Monleón [1937]

NUMBER 25

Anonymous

Bauset's poster joins a long iconographic tradition in which a heroic figure vanquishes a beast embodying spiritual or political evil. This member of the Iron Column is thus the wartime version of St. George battling the dragon.

23. OBRERO! INGRESANDO EN LA COLUMNA DE HIERRO FORTALECES LA REVOLUCION

WORKER! JOINING THE IRON COLUMN FORTIFIES THE REVOLUTION [33 x 24cm]
J. Bauset [1936?]. Issued in Valencia by the UGT/CNT.

The soldier takes a classical pose, against a formal column, but the column, we realize, is black in color, like the iron column the poster advertises. Nick Chapman offers the following analysis of the poster: "Passionate ideological militancy made the Iron Column perhaps the most widely known of the militia units other than the Durruti Column and the communists' Fifth Regiment. It was also one of the few militia units to produce its own recruitment and propaganda posters. One such poster, designed by Bauset, shows a worker holding a rifle in one hand and beckoning to the viewer with the other. His open mouth seems to utter the slogan of the poster. . . . The armed worker stands on a platform bearing the initials of the two principle anarchist organizations—the FAI and CNT. Rising up behind him on the platform is a massive column supporting a large piece of cast iron—obviously symbolizing the Iron Column. The man is shown as if seen from below and at an angle so that the image is given dynamic diagonal lines and a powerful perspective, graphically imparting a sense of heroic grandeur and purpose. The poster's caption—with its call to `fortify the revolution' and the absence of any mention of the war—clearly reflects the same position as Durruti's statement that the anarchist militias were `fighting for the revolution' and not the Republic."

24. LENTAMENTE, PERO CON ESFUERZO CONSTANTE, EL PUEBLO ESPAÑOL VA CREANDO UNA HUMANIDAD NUEVA!

SLOWLY BUT WITH CONSTANT EFFORT, THE SPANISH PEOPLE ARE CREATING A NEW HUMANITY! [36 x 26cm]
M. Monleón [1937]. Issued by the UGT/CNT in Valencia.

The statue of a naked woman was a familiar symbol of the city of Valencia, where this poster was produced. The government of the Republic was relocated from Madrid to Valencia in November of 1936. This poster was also probably printed as a cover for the magazine *Estudios*, published in Valencia.

25. AYUDA A LOS HOSPITALES DE SANGRE SUSSCRIBIENDOTE, ADQUIRIENDO NUMEROS PARA ESTA RIFA POPULAR. SELLOS Y TARJETAS POSTALES.

ASSIST THE BLOOD BANK HOSPITALS, GET YOUR TICKETS FOR THIS PEOPLE'S RAFFLE. STAMPS AND POSTCARDS.
[33 x 24cm]
Anonymous. Issued in Valencia by the CNT/AIT.

The poster was part of a fund raising campaign for wartime medical services. Small illustrated stamps sold to support a variety of causes were often quite strikingly designed. Many were the artistic equivalent of small posters. Note the stylized, flattened, and serialized elements in the poster drawn from the art deco design movement.

NUMBER 26

Juana Francisca & José Bardasano

NUMBER 27

Juan Antonio Morales [1936]

NUMBER 28

Parrilla [1937]

26. NUESTROS BRAZOS SERAN LOS VUESTROS
OUR ARMS WILL BE YOURS   [41 x 26cm]
Juana Francisca & José Bardasano. Issued by the Union of Young Women.

Juana Francisca and José Bardasano, both artists working on behalf of the Spanish Republic, were also married. The poster gives the name of the sponsoring organization in both Spanish *(Union de Muchachas)* and Catalan *(Aliança de la Dona Jove)*. The caption and image together suggest that, while the men below are away fighting, the women's arms will be extensions of the men's. In other words, the women will keep the factories running. Thus the promise reassures and builds the morale of the men at the bottom of the poster who are heading for the front.

27. LOS NACIONALES
THE NATIONALISTS   [122 x 97cm]
[Juan Antonio Morales–1936]. Issued by the Ministry of Propaganda.

On April 27, 1937, American volunteer Harry Meloff sent his friend Julius Blickstein a postcard version of this poster with the following inscription on the reverse:

The poster's cartoon-style graphics satirize the groups comprising Franco's Nationalist alliance (the Burgos Junta), with the toy-like character of the boat suggesting a ship of fools. On the right is a monocled German capitalist proudly displaying a swastika on his lapel and carrying a bag of coins. Below, a Catholic bishop (with loyalties to Rome) signals his support with a two- fingered blessing. An Italian general with a fasces on his sash mans a cannon on the left, and at the back stand two Moors, one wearing a fez and carrying a rifle. The figures peering through the three portholes appear to be Moors as well. Thus the poster suggests the Nationalist coalition is composed of foreign interests rather than native Spaniards. The boat is sailing from Lisbon, where Portugal's dictator offered Franco his support. Around its mast is wrapped a banner imprinted with Franco's slogan "Arriba España" (Spain Arise). But the mast is actually a gallows, and from the gallows a map of Spain hangs lynched. Above all this a cartoon vulture perches, cheerful about the deadly mission this group is undertaking. Nigel Glendinning suggests the prelate is Cardinal Gomá who suspended the clergy in the Basque country who supported the Republic.

The poster is unsigned. John Tisa in *The Palette and the Flame: Posters of the Spanish Civil War* attributes it to Cañavate, who did other satirical posters, but the February 28, 1938, issue of *Time* magazine has a story about Spain's posters which contains the following passage: "Most popular throughout Leftist Spain is *Los Nacionales*, a fantasy turned out in the first weeks of the war by a husky, grey-eyed cartoonist named Juan Antonio Morales, 26, who has since joined the Leftist army and was last week engaged in the fighting at Teruel."

28. LOS INTERNACIONALES—UNIDOS A LOS ESPAÑOLES, LUCHAMOS CONTRA EL INVASOR
THE INTERNATIONALS—UNITED WITH THE SPANISH WE FIGHT THE INVADER   [100 x 70cm]
Parrilla [1937]. Issued in Madrid by the InternationalBrigades.

"The general, the banker, and the priest in pink;
It won't take long for their boat to sink."

We're ready for them, kid. I'll get a crack at them mighty soon. Regards to your folks & Rose.
Salud!

NUMBER 29

Anonymous

NUMBER 30

Juan Antonio

NUMBER 31

Osmundo

In the background is the red, yellow, and purple Republican flag. Before it, standing guard over the soldiers is *La Niña Bonita*, symbol of the Second Spanish Republic. In the foreground is the cartouche of the International Brigades; above the five-pointed star symbolizing the Popular Army is the clenched– fist salute of the Popular Front. The soldier on the left is wearing a French Adrian helmet, common headgear among soldiers of the Republic, and his arm band repeats the colors of the Republic. On the right the soldier wears a beret with the three-pointed star of the International Brigades. About 40,000 people from other countries came to Spain to join the fight against fascism.

29. DURRUTI—LOS ANARQUISTAS HONRADOS ESTAN EN CONTRA DE ESA FALSA LIBERTAD QUE INVOCAN LOS COBARDES PARA ESCURRIR EL BULTO

DURRUTI—TRUE ANARCHIST ARE AGAINST THE FALSE LIBERTY INVOKED BY COWARDS TO AVOID THEIR DUTY
[100 x 70cm]
Anonymous. Issued by the Federación Ibérica de Juventudes Libertarias

Charismatic as an orator and fearless in battle, Buenaventura Durruti was perhaps the most famous anarchist of the Spanish Civil War. He died while commanding militia units in University City on the Madrid front on November 20, 1936. By then, he was already a legendary figure, a result not only of his prewar politics but also of his key role in the defense of Barcelona in the early months of the war. This poster was issued by the *Federación Ibérica de Juventudes Libertarias*, an anarchist youth organization devoted, as one would expect, to abolishing private property. A number of different posters were issued by a variety of organizations to honor Durruti and claim his image.

Among the collage of photographs at the bottom of the poster, note the female militia members at the upper left. The anarchist leader Federica Montseny is giving a speech in the photo at the upper right. Armored cars are featured in photos in the center of the collage.

30. MUJERES TRABAJAR POR LOS COMPAÑEROS QUE LUCHAN

WOMEN, WORK FOR THE COMRADES WHO FIGHT [100 x 70cm]
Juan Antonio. [Issuing organization unknown]

This stylized poster may suggest women harvesting and winnowing wheat. The chaff is being separated from the grain and the wheat mounting in golden piles to the left. This poster is, in effect, the agricultural version of no. 26.

31. EL TRANSPORTE, ES LA LLAVE DE LA SOCIALIZACION Y EL TRIUNFO DE LA REVOLUCION

TRANSPORT IS THE KEY TO SOCIALIZATION AND THE TRIUMPH OF THE REVOLUTION [100 x 70cm]
Osmundo. Issued by the CNT/FAI/AIT.

There is no exact English equivalent to the Spanish *socializacion* but it implies public ownership. Public transportation was collectivized and run by the unions after the war began. The poster is still more complicated than that, however, because it suggests that collectivization will bring agriculture and industry into a wholly harmonious relationship. The contrast between rural and metropolitan life, between country and city, was worldwide but particularly extreme in Spain, where many agricultural workers lived a wholly marginal, impoverished existence. Throughout the 1930s various

NUMBER 32

Juana Francisca

NUMBER 33

Cheché [1937]

Spanish political parties suggested they could overcome the differences between city and country and bring them into an ideal relationship. This poster is thus a wartime extension of an ongoing political debate in Spain.

Note the happy, monumentalized peasant farmers who preside over the scene like tutelary deities. The sprigs of wheat and olive on opposite sides of the poster frame a ship (named "Liberty"), trucks, buses, and a tractor, all of which flow from the medallion celebrating socialization. Collectivization and mechanization, the poster urges us to recognize, will make work easier and make all workers better off.

32. CAMPEMENTO DE UNION DE MUCHACHAS—PATROCINADO POR EL C.N. DE EDUCACION FISICA
CAMP FOR THE UNION OF YOUNG WOMEN—SPONSORED BY THE NATIONAL CONFEDERATION FOR PHYSICAL EDUCATION
[211 x 150CM]
Juana Francisca. Issued by the Ministry of Public Instruction and Health.

The international Left had organized a People's Olympics in Barcelona for the summer of 1936, in protest against the regular Olympics being held in Nazi Germany. The Barcelona events, however, were cancelled when war broke out, though some of the atheletes joined the people in their successful effort to block the military from taking control of the city. For all these reasons athletics and athletic events retained a certain political force and connotativeness throughout the war in the Republic, hence the celebration of the female javelin thrower in Juana Francisca's poster from 1937 or 1938.

33. ASTURIAS: OCTUBRE, **1934–1937.** AYUDA! A LAS FAMILIAS DE LOS COMBATIENTES DEL NORTE
ASTURIAS: OCTOBER, 1934–1937. AID THE FAMILIES OF THE FIGHTERS OF THE NORTH.   [100 x 70CM]
Cheché [1937]. Issued by Spanish Red Aid.

The Asturias are a region in Northwest Spain along the Bay of Biscay. Militantly left-wing Austurian miners staged a revolt against the government in 1934; it was suppressed by troops led by Francisco Franco, who was then acting on behalf of the Second Republic. Nonetheless, the region overwhelmingly supported the new Popular Front government after the fascist rising in 1936. Cut off from the rest of Spain by October of 1936, the Asturias and the other northern provinces fought on through the summer and fall of 1937. By the end of the third week of October, however, the region had fallen to Franco. Refugees and loyalist troops circled through France to reenter Spain, and many headed for Barcelona. This poster appears to request aid for the families of those refugees. Beneath the figure of the miner is a barbed wire fence supported by posts that form the letters "U H P." These are the initials of the rallying cry of the 1934 revolt, *Union Hermanos Proletarios!* (Proletarian Brothers Unite!). Since the Astorians in revolt were, in effect, surrounded, the barbed wire is defensive.

NUMBER 34

Artel [1937]

NUMBER 35

Rivero Gil

34. UN BORRACHO! ES UN PARÁSITO. ELIMINÉMOSLE!

A DRUNK! HE IS A PARASITE! ELIMINATE HIM! [100 x 70CM]
Artel [1937]. Issued by the Aragon Department of Public Order.

Un Borracho suggests the cubist influence on Spanish Civil War posters. In his introduction to *The Palette and the Flame* Anthony Toney makes the following comments: "Artel's counter-point of diagonals establishes a heavy sophisticated mood in his dramatically vital `Borracho' . . . Artel managed a powerful indictment. The mood is richly degenerate as symbolic innuendos are ingrained in the rhythmic diagonal thrusts that include the bottles, expressive capped head, and various captions."

35. ATENCION! LAS ENFERMEDADES VENERAS AMENAZAN TU SALUD. PREVENTE CONTRA ELLAS!

ATTENTION! VENEREAL DISEASES THREATEN YOUR HEALTH. TAKE STEPS AGAINST THEM. [70 x 48CM]
Rivero Gil. Produced for the army's health ministry.

Like the previous poster's warnings about drunkenness, posters offering warnings about venereal disease are commonplace in modern war. But this powerful and unsettling poster goes much further. Slumped against the pale, naked body of the woman behind him, the helmeted soldier is colored a uniform, coagulated deep purple; he seems not merely threatened but dead. The woman's right arm appears not so much to embrace him as to pass into his body. There, as in an x-ray or an exhumation, her hand and arm become skeletal, deadly. Meanwhile, her face, half-covered, presents a blue earring that doubles, in modernist dislocation, as an anonymous eye. The sky behind her darkens, reinforcing the suggestion that this is an archetypally fatal encounter, that woman's embrace is always fatal for a soldier.

Of all the posters in the exhibit, however, this may be the one that is most deceptive in isolation from other posters on the same subject. For although the poster is iconographically unconventional, its message to soldiers warning against the danger of prostitution—the danger to a soldier's health and thus to the success of military campaigns—is quite conventional. Indeed, there were several more posters warning soldiers about venereal disease. But a much more visible poster campaign against prostitution was waged by two women's organizations, *Mujeres Libres* and the *Secretariado Femininino del POUM*. The anti-prostitution posters issued by *Mujeres Libres* denounced prostitution as a form of slavery imposed by the bourgeoisie and urged prostitutes to take advantage of the new "centers for rehabilitation and reinstatement" established to help women find other ways to support themselves.

PART FOUR: A LINCOLN BRIGADE ALBUM

The last part of the exhibit is a photographic tribute to the men and women who brought these posters home. We include images of what the American volunteers did in Spain and what they saw there, as well as photographs of the men and women themselves. The exhibit includes photographs, contemporary statements, and selections from wartime letters. It concludes with a 5-foot wide color photograph of what may be the only wall newspaper to have survived the war intact. Brought home from the military hospital at Denia on the Mediterranean coast by Irving Goff, the original is now in the Rare Books and Special Collections Division of the University of Illinois Library. A number of the photographs on exhibit are reproduced in *Madrid 1937: Letters of the Abraham Lincoln Brigade from the Spanish Civil War*, published to coincide with the opening of *Shouts from the Wall*. Since the number of photographs displayed will depend on the space available at individual venues, we are not providing a comprehensive list of them in the catalogue.

BIBLIOGRAPHY

ALVAH BESSIE, ed. *Heart of Spain*—(New York: Veterans of the Abraham Lincoln Brigade, 1952).

JULIO ALVAREZ DEL VÁYO, *Freedom's Battle*, trans. Eileen E. Brooke —(New York: Knopf, 1940).

SANTIAGO CARRILLO, *Bardasano, Su Obra*—(Mexico: M. Leon Sanchez, 1943).

PETER N. CARROLL, *The Odyssey of the Abraham Lincoln Brigade: Americans In the Spanish Civil War*—(Stanford, Calif.: Stanford University Press, 1994).

NICHOLAS CHAPMAN, *Revolution and Counter-Revolution in Posters of the Spanish Civil War*—(Unpublished undergraduate honors' thesis, University of California at Berkeley, 1993).

JOAN FONTCUBERTA, *Josep Renau: Fotomontador*—(Mexico City: Fondo de Cultura Económica, 1984).

Carles Fontseré: Roma Paris Londres 1960—(Barcelona: Fundació Caixa de Pensions, 1984).

CARLES FONTSERÉ, *Catalan Posters of the Spanish Civil War*. In Rupert Martin and Frances Morris, eds. *No Pasaran!—Photographs and Posters of the Spanish Civil War*—(Bristol: Arnolfini Gallery, 1986).

CARLES FONTSERÉ, *El Sindicato de Dibujantes Profesionales*. In Joseph Temes, ed. *Carteles de la República y de la Guerra Civil*.

CARL GEISER, *Prisoners of the Good Fight*—(Westport, Conn.: Lawrence Hill & Company, 1986).

NIGEL GLENDINNING, *Art and the Spanish Civil War*. In Stephen M. Hart, ed. *No Pasaran!: Art, Literature and the Spanish Civil War*—(London: Tamesis Books, 1988).

CARMEN GRIMAU, *El Cartel Republicano en la Guerra Civil*—(Madrid: Ediciones Cátedra, 1979).

GABRIEL JACKSON, *A Concise History of the Spanish Civil War*—(New York: John Day, 1974).

ARTHUR H. LANDIS, *The Abraham Lincoln Brigade*—(New York: Citadel Press, 1967).

JAVIER GÓMEZ LÓPEZ, ed. *Catálogo de Carteles de la República y la Guerra Civil Españolas en la Biblioteca Nacional*—(Madrid: Ministry of Culture, 1990).

LUIS MARÍA CARUNCHO AMAT AND CAROLINA PEÑA BARDASANO, eds. *Bardasano* (1910– 1979)—(Madrid: Artes Gráficas Municipales, 1986).

Cary Nelson, ed. *Remembering Spain: Hemingway's Civil War Eulogy and the Veterans of the Abraham Lincoln Brigade*—(Urbana: University of Illinois Press, 1994).

Cary Nelson and Jefferson Hendricks, eds. *Madrid 1937: Letters of the Abraham Lincoln Brigade from the Spanish Civil War*—(New York: Routledge, 1996).

Josep Renau, *Fata Morgana USA: The American Way of Life*—(Valencia: Museum of Photographic Arts, 1991).

Josep Renau, *Función Social del Cartel*—(Valencia: Fernando Torres, 1976).

Edwin Rolfe, *Collected Poems*, ed. Cary Nelson and Jefferson Hendricks —(Urbana: University of Illinois Press, 1993).

Robert A. Rosenstone, *Crusade of the Left: The Lincoln Battalion in the Spanish Civil War*—(New York: Pegasus, 1969).

Josefina Serván Corchero and Antonio Trinidad Muñoz, *Las Mujeres en la Cartelística de la Guerra Civil*. In *Las Mujeres y la Guerra Civil Española*—(Salamanca: Ministry of Culture, 1991).

Manfred Schmidt, ed. *Josep Renau: Grafik und Fotomontagen*—(East Berlin: Staatlicher Kunsthandel der DDR, 1981).

Josep Temes, ed. *Carteles de la República y de la Guerra Civil*—(Barcelona: La Gaya Ciencia, 1978).

Hugh Thomas, *The Spanish Civil War*—(Revised and enlarged edition, New York: Harper and Row, 1977).

John Tisa, *The Palette and the Flame: Posters of the Spanish Civil War*—(New York: International Publishers, 1979).

Josephina Alix Trueba, ed. *Pabellón Español: Exposicion Internacional de París 1937*—(Madrid: Ministry of Culture, 1987).

Kathleen Vernon, ed. *The Spanish Civil War and the Visual Arts*—(Ithaca: Center for International Studies, Cornell University, 1990).

Milton Wolff, *Another Hill: An Autobiographical Novel about the Spanish Civil War*—(Urbana: University of Illinois Press, 1994).